THE ACTION HERO'S HANDBOOK

The
ACTION
HERO'S
Handbook

*How to Catch a Great White Shark,
Perform the Vulcan Nerve Pinch,
Track a Fugitive, and Dozens of Other
TV and Movie Skills*

by David Borgenicht and
Joe Borgenicht

MICHAEL JOSEPH
an imprint of
PENGUIN BOOKS

MICHAEL JOSEPH

Published by the Penguin Group
Penguin Books Ltd, 80 Strand, London WC2R 0RL, England
Penguin Putnam Inc., 375 Hudson Street, New York, New York 10014, USA
Penguin Books Australia Ltd., 250 Camberwell Road,
Camberwell, Victoria 3124, Australia
Penguin Books Canada Ltd, 10 Alcorn Avenue, Toronto, Ontario, Canada M4V 3B2
Penguin Books India (P) Ltd, 11 Community Centre,
Panchsheel Park, New Delhi – 110 017, India
Penguin Books (NZ) Ltd, Cnr Rosedale and Airborne Roads,
Albany, Auckland, New Zealand
Penguin Books (South Africa) (Pty) Ltd, 24 Sturdee Avenue,
Rosebank 2196, South Africa

Penguin Books Ltd, Registered Offices: 80 Strand, London WC2R 0RL, England

www.penguin.com

First published in the United States of America by Quirk Books 2002
First Published in Great Britain by Michael Joseph 2002

Copyright © Quirk Productions, Inc., 2002

Typeset by
Frances Soo Ping Chow
Printed in Singapore
by Tien Wah Press

A CIP catalogue record for this book is available from the British Library

ISBN 0-718-14550-X

CONTENTS

Chapter Five: Escape Skills . . . 140

INTRODUCTION

Action heroes are made, not born. Even those with superpowers and precocious talents had to start somewhere. After all, did you really think that Superman could always leap tall buildings in a single bound, that James Bond always knew to drink martinis shaken (not stirred), or that Indiana Jones was born with a whip in his hand instead of a rattle? Of course not—every action hero shows a clear aptitude for heroism, but needs guidance along the way.

In the beginning, every action hero is just an ordinary but good man or woman. The hero must first identify and then hone his skills and talents. Then, before he achieves hero status, he'll have to overcome a series of obstacles (physical, emotional, or paranormal). And somehow, through the cumulative effect of his upbringing (good or bad), formative life experiences, an apprenticeship, and the occasional bite of a radioactive insect, his inner action hero eventually comes to the surface.

But even after he's saved his first dude or damsel in distress, or thwarted his first plot for world domination, there are times when the most accomplished action heroes still need a little help. No man or woman is an island—and this applies to secret agents, hot private detectives in cat suits, capable Vulcans and Jedi Knights, and rugged archaeologists alike.

That's where this book comes in. This book truly is your guide to keeping up with the Indiana Joneses. It's the *only* primer on the essential skills all action heroes *must know* to survive and thrive in this dangerous world—Good Guy Skills, Love Skills, Paranormal Skills, Fighting Skills, Escape Skills—all from real experts in the subject at hand.

The skills we teach have all been featured in television shows and movies. But before now you've never been able to read a real-world, step-by-step, how-to guide to these skills. Let us reiterate: all of the information in this book is completely real. Want to know how to *really* catch a great white shark? To actually deliver a Vulcan Nerve Pinch? To spyproof your hotel room? To win a fight when outnumbered? To climb down Mount Rushmore National Monument? It's all inside. We spoke with FBI agents, sexologists, stuntmen, hypnotists, karate masters, criminologists, detectives, and dozens of other highly trained professionals to obtain real-world solutions to the kinds of situations that usually only happen to people with very cool names, unusually tight clothing, and few (if any) sweat glands.

So use the information wisely—and whatever you do, don't let this book fall into the wrong hands.

Read on, and good luck—we're counting on you.

—The Authors

CHAPTER 1
Good Guy Skills

THE MOST BASIC SKILLS an action hero needs are commonly referred to as "good guy skills." These are the abilities needed to protect yourself from your enemies as you set off on your mission—whether you're entering a hotel room, driving a bus that has been turned into a bomb, or being held hostage in a Los Angeles skyscraper. You need these skills to protect yourself first, then to save others, and finally to catch the bad guys.

Before you start your training, you should decide how you like to work. Are you a loner, or would you rather have a buddy along? Are you a veteran, or do you need rookie guidance? Would you rather be in the line of fire or in the line at the wedding? Once you've answered these questions, you'll better understand your limitations and be able to select which skills best apply to the situation at hand.

So read on and learn—it's a dangerous world out there, but with the skills you'll master in this section, you should be able to make it out alive.

Nude Female Assassin (Luciana Paluzzi): *Aren't you in the wrong room, Mr. Bond?*

James Bond (Sean Connery): *Not from where I'm standing.*
  —Thunderball

The first stop on your mission is often the hotel where you'll be staying—but unfortunately, the hotel room is where the traveling action hero is often most exposed. And no matter what the movies suggest, you can't always expect an intruder to be a scantily clad femme fatale or Brad Pitt–type who wants to engage in a bit of preexecution lovemaking—thereby conveniently giving you the opportunity to sway her or his allegiance. (Although it does happen that way from time to time.) Be aware: maintenance and hotel workers regularly gain access to your room—and thus, so can your enemies. With that in mind, here's what to do, according to Shawn Engbrecht of the Center for Advanced Security Studies.

ENTERING THE ROOM

Ideally, you should be prepared to use some sort of implement (blunt object, weapon) in case you interrupt the intruder. Carry a flashlight or night vision goggles so that you won't need to fumble for light switches as you enter the room.

Step 1: Stand toward the hinge side of the doorframe, not in the center or on the side with the doorknob.

This stance will protect you from an attack immediately upon entry, or from a gun fired at the door from inside the room.

PRE-ARRIVAL AND ARRIVAL TIPS

▪ **Reserve several rooms under several different names.**
Using several aliases can make it difficult for your enemy to know which room to invade. Play the shell game—stay in a different room every other night (or so).

▪ **Reserve your room(s) on at least the sixth or seventh floor of the hotel.**
This will make it difficult for anything to be thrown into your room from the ground. Avoid cabana-style hotels that are only on ground level—ground floor entry is the easiest to gain.

▪ **Try to obtain rooms on a side of the hotel that stands higher than the other buildings.**
Avoid staying in a room that has other rooms overlooking it, which could make it easier for someone to gain entry through a window or balcony, keep tabs on you from across the way, or give a sniper a good angle.

▪ **Never use the hotel's main entrance and avoid using the main elevators or stairs.**
Use service entrances, exits, and freight elevators as frequently as possible. If you can't use those, try to enter and exit the hotel through an underground garage, side or pool entrance, delivery door, or kitchen. Avoid the hotel lobby whenever possible.

Step 2: Throw the door open quickly and forcefully so that it hits the wall behind it.

You'll quickly discover whether someone is standing directly behind the door. Either the door will not open all the way or you will obtain audible evidence of the intruder's existence.

Step 3: Leave the door open until you have cleared the room.

If someone is inside, it's always better to give him a way out to avoid a confrontation. You should, however, be ready for confrontation at a moment's notice (see "How to Be Ready for Anything," p. 130, and "How to Disarm a Thug with a Gun," p. 137).

Step 4: Enter the room with your back to the wall nearest to the entry door.

This will make you less of an easy target.

Draw curtains before passing windows.

Quickly scan the room.

Keep your back against the wall.

Leave the door open until you have cleared the room.

Check behind doors and under beds.

Step 5: **Keeping your back against the wall, move quickly around the perimeter of the room, scanning up and down and from side to side.**

Move clockwise around the room, entering bedrooms, bathrooms, and closets as you come to them. Open the doors as in steps 1 and 2 and secure each room in turn.

You may need to use a flashlight or night vision goggles to check these spaces. If you use night vision goggles, be sure to keep one eye free. If the goggles are exposed to a light source, the resulting "white out" will render you temporarily blind.

Step 6: **If you are about to pass by windows, draw the curtains before you pass.**

Continue with your sweep until you are back where you started.

Step 7: **Next, check out any potential hiding places.**

The most common hiding places are under the bed(s) and in closets and showers.

Step 8: **Look for surveillance devices.**

Today's miniature technology makes it very difficult to find high-tech bugs, but a basic sweep may turn up a listening device or two. Check under lampshades and lamp bases, under furniture, inside the heating or air-conditioning units, in the telephone receiver, and on the telephone line. Look for anything out of the ordinary. Simple devices, like the traditional "round bug in the receiver," will be easy to recognize, but are very rarely used by sophisticated eavesdroppers.

WARNING SYSTEMS

- **When inside the room, create a perimeter warning system.**
Place an empty glass bottle or a stack of empty cans about two inches inside the front door and in front of each window. Any intruder will knock these over upon entering and warn you of his approach.

- **When leaving the room, use these simple but effective surveillance techniques:**

  - **Open the drawer or door that you want to protect. Wedge a folded match in the gap between it and its frame, and close the drawer or door.**

  - **Place a small piece of tape across the outside of the door you want to protect and its frame, near the lower corner.**

  - **Stretch a strand of your hair across the door and the frame and attach it using a heavy dose of saliva.**

If any of the items have become detached or have moved, you'll know that someone has been inside (or is still there).

Inspector Jacques Clouseau (Peter Sellers): *Facts, Hercule, facts! Nothing matters but the facts. Without them the science of criminal investigation is nothing more than a guessing game.*
   —*A Shot in the Dark*

The basic rule for securing a crime scene is "safety first." So when you arrive on the scene, be sure the area is secure—for yourself, for any victims and survivors, and for any evidence. You have to make sure that your bible-spouting serial killer or "retired" cat burglar has left the scene and is now watching you from the safety of the building across the street. Next, you must determine what evidence has been left behind. According to Locard's Theory of Evidence, regardless of how careful the criminal has been, he will always leave some evidence behind. Here's what to do, according to crime lab manager George Throckmorton.

SECURING THE SCENE

It's always best to work with backup. But if a victim's life is at stake, you will have to act fast—and perhaps alone.

Step 1: Check the area to make sure the criminal is no longer present.
   A crime scene is not a crime scene unless the perpetrator has left or been apprehended. If the perpetrator is still present, then it is a crime in progress. If you are indoors, secure the room (see "How to Secure/Spyproof a Hotel Room," p. 12). If you are outdoors, cordon off the area from other foot or vehicle traffic. Park a car or tape off the area in front of the crime scene.

Step 2: Check the victim (if there is a victim), and apply life-saving medical assistance, if necessary.

If the victim is conscious and in good health, take him to an adjacent area, outside the crime scene, to be interviewed—a nearby hallway or side street, for example. If he is unconscious, check for a pulse and for breathing. If you cannot rouse the victim, call the paramedics. If the victim is dead, do not touch anything more than you need to determine that.

Step 3: DO NOT TOUCH ANYTHING!

And keep everyone else from touching, walking on, or otherwise disturbing the area.

READING THE SCENE

Step 1: Determine what the crime is.

After securing the scene but before touching anything more, determine what the crime is. Are there witnesses present who can explain what happened? Is there broken glass at the window and an alarm sounding? Is there a body or an injured victim? Determine as best you can what happened and where it took place—perhaps a bag of uncut diamonds was stolen from a safe and a few were left behind, or someone was killed in the kitchen by a Cuisinart blade.

Step 2: Begin to think like the criminal.

As you observe the area think about how you would have committed the crime. Where would your point of entry be? What tools or weapons would you use? What would you have done if your victim put up a struggle?

Step 3: If the crime scene is indoors, find the point of entry.

Logically, if a crime took place *inside*, then the criminal must have gotten in. From the *outside* of the building, check the windows and doors. If no marks or broken glass can be found, then you can assume that the criminal had a key or was invited in or expected. If you find a scratch or mark of any kind on a doorknob or hinge or broken glass at an open window, then you have found evidence of forced entry.

Step 4: Process the point of entry.

Take a wide-angle photo of the point of entry, and then examine the doorframe, lock, window, and knob for evidence. Take close-up photos of any marks or scratches and measure them to determine what kind of tool was used to gain entry. A small flathead screwdriver can make a long, scratching mark. But its mark would not be as consistently straight as one created with a wider screwdriver or a knife. Look for the smallest possible example of a tool's mark.

Step 5: Look for obvious evidence.

As a general rule the more serious the crime, the more evidence you should gather. Richard Saferstein, author of *Criminalistics: An Introduction to Forensic Science*, defines evidence as "any and all objects that can establish that a crime has been committed or can provide a link between a crime and its victim or a crime and its perpetrator." Unless a witness can tell you what objects are out of place, assume that everything at a crime scene is evidence. Start your search outside, then move to the inside. Begin by looking for the obvious clues—blood, footprints, grease marks, cigarette butts, or anything that looks out of place. Then start looking for less obvious or readily visible clues—hair, threads, or fingerprints.

Take photographs of all suspected evidence before you disturb it, then carefully collect the evidence. Always wear gloves and pick up evidence with tweezers or another object—a rag or cloth—if your equipment is elsewhere. Place the evidence in a sealed container or bag to avoid contamination.

Step 6: Look for signs of a struggle.

Is there broken or disturbed furniture, broken glass, or another disturbed object? If so, a struggle may have taken place. Process as evidence any object that may have been involved in the struggle.

Find point of entry.

Look for signs of struggle.

Collect evidence.

Look for weapons.

Do not disturb body.

Collect prints.

Step 7: Once you have found something that qualifies as evidence, search near that item for other evidence.

Look for surfaces from which you might be able to lift a fingerprint—the smoother the better. Look for a weapon or dropped clue—cigarettes or personal effects that may have fallen out of the perpetrator's pocket. Check in the garbage cans, under tables, or under the victim.

Step 8: Try to reconstruct the crime in your head.

Judging from the evidence you have found—point of entry, signs of a struggle, dropped weapons, or other clues—put together a theory of what happened. Then begin processing the evidence.

Step 9: Examine the evidence.

Scrutinize the evidence for obvious characteristics: scratches, marks, or other identifying traits that may indicate where the object came from and how it was used. Process the evidence for fingerprints (see "How to Take Fingerprints," p. 24).

Step 10: Juxtapose the crime scene evidence against evidence taken from your prime suspects.

For example, a fingerprint from the scene should be compared against a fingerprint from the suspect, or a boot print from the scene with the suspect's boot. Use a magnifying glass to look for matches in the general characteristics (e.g., same patterns, treads, etc.). If they match, look more closely for matches in individual characteristics (e.g., same scratches, marks, and tears).

The truly careful bad guy will roll up his pant legs, clean the area,
and try to alter or eliminate evidence of his crime.

HOW BAD GUYS COVER UP THEIR CRIMES

The problem bad guys encounter in cleaning up a crime scene is that the longer they spend at the scene, the more evidence they leave; the more they clean, the more likely they will leave behind more evidence. Here's what they actually do, courtesy of Utah State Crime Lab's supervising criminalist, Kevin Patrick.

- Alter evidence of entry

  To prevent accurate identification and measurement of their tool, the crook will use the same tool—crowbar, screwdriver, and so on—to scratch out the marks he left. If he has broken a glass door or window to gain entry, he will check the glass for strands of cloth or thread his clothing may have left behind and discard the incriminating shards.

- Wipe down surfaces

  The bad guy will use a soft cloth to eliminate or make unreadable fingerprints from the entry door and doorknobs, drawers, windows and latches, telephones, glasses, and so forth.

- Clean up the evidence

  The truly obsessive crook will roll up his pant legs, mop the floors, vacuum the carpet, and clean blood or "struggle" stains with bleach. He'll dispose of any evidence—broken objects, glass, or anything else he touched—by carrying it away and dumping it far from the crime scene.

Note: While cleaning may help cover the surface evidence of the crime, the bad guys inevitably leave more for you to find. Check unusually clean floors for footprints. Check the vacuum bag for traces of the vacuumed evidence. Investigate spots on the carpet that don't quite match the rest—bleached-out blood stains will actually settle out of the carpet and transfer valuable DNA evidence onto the floor below.

HOW TO
TAKE FINGERPRINTS

Vivian Sternwood (Lauren Bacall): *So, you're a private detective. I didn't know they existed, except in books.*
  —The Big Sleep

Even the most careful criminals often leave fingerprints behind. But you can't count on it being easy to find those prints—criminals may wear gloves or meticulously wipe down the scene before they escape. And then there will be those times when you will want to take prints from a crime scene but have, alas, forgotten your Official Detective Fingerprinting Kit. Take heart—according to crime lab manager George Throckmorton, the creative action hero can still capture solid fingerprints from a crime scene even without a kit, simply by using his own ingenuity (and a few easy-to-find materials).

Note: Always wear gloves when processing evidence for fingerprints.

PENCIL AND FEATHER METHOD

What You'll Need
- Transparent tape
- An index card or piece of paper
- A pencil
- A feather or brush
- A coin
- A knife, screwdriver, or other sharp implement

Step 1: Look for potential fingerprint-bearing objects.

The smoother the surface, the better the fingerprint. Prints can be secured from almost any surface, but better prints may be found on the following surfaces:

- Glass
- Painted surfaces
- Metal
- Linoleum
- Woods with smooth, varnished surfaces
- Paper

Step 2: Grind the lead from your pencil into a fine graphite powder.

With a sharp object—knife, screwdriver, or the like—break the lead from the pencil into tiny pieces. Lay the pieces on a table or other flat surface. Using a coin, grind the pieces until you have a fine powder.

Step 3: Lay your object on a table so that it lies as flat as possible.

Step 4: Sprinkle the powder onto the surface of your object.

Step 5: With your feather, lightly dust the powder off the surface to reveal the fingerprint.

The powder will hold onto the oils from the suspect's skin, and you should be able to see the print take shape. Brush very lightly—otherwise, you may dust away the fingerprint. (Note: If your powder is not particularly fine, you can blow the graphite off with a quick breath of air.)

Step 6: Transfer the fingerprint to a card.

Hold a small strip of transparent tape from both ends and place it

Pencil and Feather Fingerprinting Method

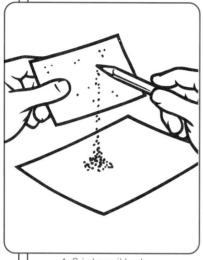

1. Grind pencil lead into fine powder.

2. Sprinkle powder onto surface.

3. Lightly dust surface to reveal print.

4. Use tape to transfer print.

over the fingerprint. Press it down for a moment, then carefully pull the tape up from one edge. The fingerprint will transfer onto the tape. Stick the tape facedown onto your card. Follow the instructions for "Reading Fingerprints" (p. 28).

SUPERGLUE AND MATCH METHOD

What You'll Need
- Superglue
- A piece of foil (about 6" x 6")
- A match
- An index card or piece of paper

Step 1: After you have found the object you wish to fingerprint, form the foil into a small bowl and place about one teaspoon of superglue into the foil.

Step 2: Place the object so that it is suspended over the edge of a table.
Place the object so that the surface you want to fingerprint is facedown, just past the edge of the table. If you cannot rest the object easily on the table, you may have to have a gloved associate hold it just so.

Step 3: Hold the foil about three inches below the evidence.

Step 4: Light the match and hold it under the foil.
As the superglue heats up, the fumes attach themselves to the evidence and leave a sharp, white film defining the fingerprint. This process works most effectively when the evidence and superglue fumes are in a confined space together, so the closer you can hold the heating glue to the evidence, the better.

Step 5: As on page 25, transfer the fingerprint to a card.

READING FINGERPRINTS

What You'll Need
- An inkpad
- A blank sheet of paper
- A magnifying glass

Step 1: Take your suspect's fingerprints by pressing each of his fingers in turn to an inkpad.

Step 2: Press each inked finger to a plain sheet of paper.

As you press, firmly roll the suspect's finger from side to side. This will give you a complete print.

Step 3: Juxtapose your suspect's prints with the fingerprints you lifted at the scene.

Place one of your suspect's prints side by side with a crime scene print.

Step 4: Examine the fingerprints.

With a magnifying glass, try to determine the print's class characteristics. If both prints are an arch, loop, or whorl, proceed to compare individual characteristics. If the class characteristics do not agree, look for another fingerprint match.

If both prints—facing in the same direction—have the same bifurcations, ridge endings, ridge dots, or enclosures, you have a fingerprint match.

U.S. Marshal Gerard (Tommy Lee Jones): *What I want out of each and every one of you is a hard target search of every gas station, residence, warehouse, farmhouse, henhouse, outhouse, and doghouse in that area. . . . Your fugitive's name is Dr. Richard Kimble. Go get him.*
  —*The Fugitive*

According to Kevin R. Hackie's California School of Bail Enforcement *Fugitive Apprehension Manual*, tracking a fugitive effectively is generally a matter of placing yourself in the fugitive's shoes and then following relentlessly in her footsteps until you can predict her next move and finally head her off at the pass. The best way to find someone is to gather as much information about her as you can, and then use that information to lead you to more information, and so on, and so on—until you trap her on the roof (or the edge of the cliff)—where there's no way out but straight down. Just hope she doesn't have the guts to jump.

Step 1: Adopt an alias.

In most cases, you will receive more assistance from people if you work undercover. Never identify yourself as a law enforcement agent, private investigator, or bounty hunter. Instead, approach your subjects as if you were an old friend, relative, or employer of the fugitive. (See p. 32 for "How to Interrogate a Suspect.")

Step 2: Go to the fugitive's last place of residence.

Under the cover of being an old friend, talk to her landlord or family members about any plans she may have let slip to them. Stake out the neighborhood mailman and ask for the fugitive's forwarding address.

Step 3: Go through the trash.

Under the cover of casually looking for recyclable materials, you can usually get through someone's trash unnoticed. Because of limited time and space, a fugitive on the run will usually only take things of immediate value—clothes, money, and the like. But the information she leaves behind in her trash is a treasure to you. Take her trash back to your own home or office, where you can sift through it away from neighbors' prying eyes. Look for phone bills, letters from family, evidence of aliases—anything you can find that may hold a clue. Check out her magazine subscriptions to get an idea of hobbies and interests—what your fugitive might be doing in her spare time.

Step 4: Contact her former employer.

Posing as a potential employer checking references, try to obtain information from former employers and co-workers. A fugitive often will let plans slip to a co-worker. Check with the payroll department to see if she left a forwarding address.

Step 5: Check public records.

A call to the county clerk of the town where your fugitive last resided can turn up records of divorce, property tax liens, civil suits, voter registration, aliases, and other information that may hold valuable clues to her current whereabouts and identity.

Step 6: Go to the residences or workplaces of former lovers or spouses.

An upfront questioning of ex-lovers or ex-spouses may turn up some helpful information—especially if they have been wronged. If they are not helpful, be suspicious and undertake surveillance on them. They may be protecting or even sheltering your fugitive. Check them out as you would the fugitive, using the methods in steps 3 to 5.

FUGITIVE HUNTER'S TIPS

- **Use reverse phone directories or Internet search engines (available at most phone company Web sites) to look up phone numbers and addresses and attach them to names.**
  With a phone number, these companies can give you names and addresses of occupants. With an address, you can get phone numbers and names.

- **Protect your sources.**
  To retain your sources inside police departments, DMVs, credit bureaus, etc., you must never reveal them to anyone.

- **Earn your favors.**
  Many of the people you come in contact with during your search may be looking for your fugitive as well. She may owe them money or have wronged them in another way. They may agree to help you, but you should be willing to do them favors in return. Offer to turn the fugitive's information over to your contacts after you find her or to look for another of your contact's delinquents at no cost.

Step 7: **Try to obtain private information through moles, contacts, or friends.**

Information from police departments, the department of motor vehicles, the post office, airlines, credit bureaus, banks, and telephone companies will be difficult to obtain unless you are a government official or licensed authority—or if people think you are. A little confidence and a convincing cover story (along with the occasional palm greasing) can go a long way. Friends and contacts at these various institutions may voluntarily provide you with this information. (After all, you *are* tracking the bad guy.)

If you have a contact at a bank or credit bureau who can run a credit check, you may turn up information about which credit cards your fugitive had applied for and/or uses. When you determine which cards your fugitive may have, contact the company's security division. They will have access to the latest charges, purchase locations, and so forth.

HOW TO INTERROGATE A SUSPECT

Detective Nick Curran (Michael Douglas): *You like playing games don't you?*
Catherine Tramell (Sharon Stone) (recrosses her legs and adjusts
  her position in the chair): *I have a degree in psychology, it goes with the turf.*
  Games are fun.
    —Basic Instinct

Unfortunately, questioning a suspect isn't always like it is in the movies—only rarely do your suspects turn out to be hot blondes with a disdain for undergarments. According to Detective Chip Morgan, when questioning a suspect it's important to keep things simple and direct. Try to read the subject's personality—would a friendly or aggressive approach serve you best? Do you want to keep her sitting in a hot room under a hot light for hours before beginning your questioning, or make her feel comfortable? Listen carefully and watch your subject's behavior for clues. Watch your subject's lower body as well—you never know when you'll get lucky.

Step 1: **Before you begin questioning or even approach your subject, review all available information.**
   Gather and review any case files, witness accounts, or other information you have about the suspect. During the interview, be prepared to evaluate and reevaluate all the information in your head, always asking yourself, "Do the suspect's answers jibe with the evidence, witness accounts, and crime scene evaluation?"

Step 2: **Set clear goals for the interview—information, interpretation, or confession.**
   Are you questioning a witness, an accessory, or a criminal? In each case you must set a different goal. If you are interviewing a witness

for information, then your goal is to obtain her version of the facts. If you are interviewing an accessory or a criminal, then your goal is to extract a confession. Set a goal of obtaining the answer to one simple question for each round of interrogation so that each piece of information leads to another.

Step 3: **When interrogating a suspect, first have her relate her version of the event in her own words.**

Do not interrupt the first retelling—simply let her spin her yarn. You will undoubtedly identify holes in her story, but don't point these out yet—just take it all in. Be sure to record and/or take thorough notes of the interrogation.

Step 4: **Watch the suspect closely at all times for changes in language, stuttering or stammering, and for other nonverbal clues of stress or discomfort.**

Look for a "tell"—an unconscious gesture, expression, or verbal tic that can often indicate stress or lying. Common tells include scratching, twitching, shifting, and rapid breathing. Looking to the left is also thought to be a tell indicative of "creating" or lying, whereas looking to the right is thought to be "remembering."

Step 5: **Inject some stress into the interview by reviewing the suspect's story again, step by step.**

Again, watch closely for verbal and nonverbal cues. Mix relevant and irrelevant questions to throw her off balance, and review the story out of sequence. If she is reciting from a memorized story, it will be harder for her to jump in and out of events.

As you are questioning her, ask yourself whether the facts jibe with your suspect's story. Does her story make sense? Is it logical? Did the suspect exhibit any change in nonverbal behavior when you applied some stress? If you have identified a few

Common "Tells"

Shifting uncomfortably.

Looking away.

Scratching.

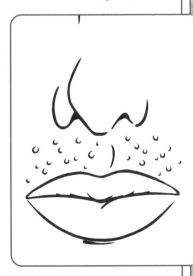

Sweating.

aspects of your suspect's story that elicited a heightened stress response, you are ready to attempt to break the suspect down.

Step 6: Accuse the suspect of the crime in question.

Make direct eye contact as you accuse her, then offer your suspect a way to "save face" and rationalize her crime. Did she need to steal for survival? Was it a violent act of passion? Does she feel badly about what she did? Suggest to her that her genuine remorse will make it much easier for you to cut a deal.

Step 7: You have your guilty party if the suspect starts to negotiate with you.

If the suspect offers you information about a "bigger fish" in exchange for more lenient punishment, she is either the perpetrator or an accessory. She must have information about the crime in question to make a deal of any kind.

Step 8: If the suspect does not readily admit to the crime, remind her of the three principles of the criminal justice system.

Three extenuating circumstances may help ameliorate her punishment:

- Does she admit guilt or remorse?
- Does she pose a continuing threat to society?
- Is she willing to make restitution?

If she does not confess, these three principles may lead a judge or jury to impose a more punishing sentence.

Step 9: If you cannot extract a confession and have no legal means of detaining her, you may have to let the suspect go.

Be sure to let the suspect know that you'll be keeping an eye on her. Give her your contact information just in case there's anything she "forgot" to tell you.

HOW TO SURVIVE IN PRISON WHEN YOU'RE WRONGLY INCARCERATED

"Red" Redding (Morgan Freeman): *Why'd you do it?*
Andy Dufresne (Tim Robbins): *I didn't, since you asked.*
Red: *You're going to fit right in. Everyone in here is innocent. Didn't you know that?*
    —*The Shawshank Redemption*

Wrongfully imprisoned action heroes rarely have the time to wait for an appeal. Often, the fate of a loved one or the free world itself is at stake if you do not get out, and so any experienced action hero knows that a dramatic rescue, a prison break, or a pardon will almost certainly be coming in time for Act III. Until that happens, however, when wrongfully incarcerated, your mission is simple: STAY ALIVE. You will need to know how to protect yourself from other prisoners, guards, evil wardens, the showers, and the food. And while no prison is the same, the same general rules for survival apply no matter where you're incarcerated—and they come from wrongfully incarcerated former prisoner Mike Pardue.

Step 1: Do not attempt an escape unless absolutely necessary.
   If you attempt an escape you put yourself at even greater risk of injury. Additionally, even if you are innocent of the crime for which you were convicted, you will still be guilty of attempting escape; if caught, time will be added to your sentence. Only when lives or the future of the free world are at stake should you attempt to break out on your own.

Step 2: Mind your own business.

As a general rule, see no evil, speak no evil, and hear no evil. Keep to yourself.

Step 3: Be the person everyone expects you to be.

If you are imprisoned for murder, then behave as a murderer. For the most part, hope that others will stay away from you because they know of your violent past. After some time you will earn the respect of your fellow inmates as they notice that no one messes with you.

Step 4: Do whatever you have to do.

If you are not getting the respect you need to stay alive and well, take whatever measures you need to survive:

- Become a dealer and provide other inmates with whatever they need.
- Take on a boyfriend or girlfriend and have him or her take care of you.
- Find out who really runs the show and befriend them.
- Try to obtain prison "currency" (porn, cigarettes, etc.) that can be used to get special treatment from fellow inmates and guards.
- Become a police informant and enter protective custody.

HOW TO CATCH A GREAT WHITE SHARK

Chief Brody (Roy Scheider): *We're gonna need a bigger boat.*
  —Jaws

These days, it's illegal to actually catch a great white shark—they are protected around the world as an endangered species. Nevertheless, as every action hero knows, dire situations do crop up, and sometimes extreme measures become necessary. According to shark hunter Douglas Mizzi, the best way to catch a great white does *not* involve chaining a chunk of meat to the end of a pier. You must learn your shark's behavior patterns, the timing of the tides, how to gaff the shark—and then, when all else fails, how to implode the oxygen tank in its mouth just before your ship sinks.

Step 1: Obtain a large boat—at least 25 feet long—and a small crew.
Great white sharks can easily reach lengths of 18 feet, so a 15-foot boat just won't do. The smallest boat you should use is a 25-footer (for a smaller shark of, say, 15 feet long or 2,600 pounds). However, ideally, you want your boat to be twice as long as your shark. Your boat should be motorized, with chairs and fishing gear (including rods, gaffing poles, and a power head) on hand. Never hunt a large shark alone. Gather a crew of at least two other deckhands.

Step 2: Learn the tides and time your trip accordingly.
When you set sail, plan to be in position about two hours before the change to low tide. Large sharks can be active throughout the day, but when the tide changes from high to low, sharks are more

active. This is when they hunt for food, and when you are most likely to catch one.

Step 3: Lay a trail of chum.

Dump buckets of fish chunks, tuna oil, chicken pellets, and animal blood into the water to set a course by which the shark can find you. Make sure you are constantly dumping your chum—your trail should be several miles long and unbroken, so that the shark will not lose his way to your hook.

If you do not have chum, look for evidence of shark feeding. If you spot a large dead fish, a great white can often be found nearby.

Step 4: Set your tackle.

Bait a large hook with a 50-pound chunk of tuna and trail it in the water. At minimum, use a 130-pound line and a 7-foot, 6-inch rod. The shorter the rod, the easier your fish will be to land. Set the drag on the reel at around 60 pounds—this will release pressure on the line before it breaks.

Step 5: Wait for the shark to take the bait.

As you troll through the water, remember that patience is a virtue, especially when shark hunting. Tell stories, jokes, or tall tales. But stay on your toes! The shark may hit at any time.

Step 6: When the shark takes the bait, set your hook.

Wind the line quickly until it's taut, then pull up sharply on your rod to set the hook in the shark's jaws. You may have to repeat this action several times or even rebait your hook and put it back out several times before you get your fish on the line.

When the hook is set, be prepared for your reel to start spinning rapidly as the shark attempts to swim away. You may need to douse the reel with water to keep it from getting hot.

Step 7: Using a pump-and-wind technique, reel the shark to the boat.

Pull the rod back toward you. The shark will fight you the entire way, so stay strong.

Quickly lower the rod tip to create some slack in the line, simultaneously reeling in about three feet of line. Continue the pump-and-wind technique throughout the fight so that the shark has little opportunity to break free. Repeat this action as necessary until the shark is near the boat. Have plenty of backup help and water on hand as it may take several hours to get the shark into this position.

Step 8: Kill the shark before bringing it aboard.

Using a gaffing pole, hold the shark in the water next to the boat. Then, using a power head—a specially designed bullet canister attached to a pole—shoot the shark in the head. *Make sure the shark is dead before pulling it into the boat!* Gaff the shark with several hooks or poles.

If you cannot kill the shark in the water, do not bring it onboard—tie it to a mount on the side of the boat using a length of cable leader and tow the shark to shore.

Pull the rod back, then lower the tip to create slack and quickly reel in the line.

HOW TO TELL
WHEN SOMEONE IS
REALLY DEAD

Leonard "Bones" McCoy (DeForest Kelley): *He's dead, Jim.*
   —Star Trek

Dead Bad Guy Rule Number One: Never assume your bad guy is dead just because he's lying immobile on the ground. Whether you're dealing with a psycho you've filled with a barrage of bullets, an android assassin you've torched with a tanker of exploding gasoline, or an obsessive blonde you've drowned after she cooked the family rabbit, you must always have proof that your enemy is really dead before you decide to turn your back and celebrate. According to Andrew J. Michaels, M.D., M.P.H., F.A.C.S., a thorough examination will always find the fakers—the ones who are just dying to come back for one more sequel.

Step 1: Poke the alleged corpse with a sharp stick or rod.
Begin with a few jabs in the side with a sharp stick. If he is faking, then you will have a weapon and some distance between you. If there is no reaction to a few sharp jabs, proceed to the next step.

Step 2: Check for breathing.
Hold a mirror or small glass up to the alleged corpse's nose and mouth for at least three minutes. If the corpse is breathing, then the mirror or glass will fog up. If there is no apparent breath, proceed to the next step.

Step 3: Check for a pulse.

Lightly apply two fingers to the area just to the side of the windpipe. Alternatively, apply two fingers to the groove on the thumb side of the underside of the wrist. Feel for a pulse.

Step 4: Check for pupil reaction to light.

Hold a flashlight up to the presumed corpse's open eyes. If his pupils get larger or smaller in reaction to light, he's not dead yet.

Step 5: Check for blinking.

Open his eyes and rub a piece of cloth or clothing across the "dead" person's eyeball. If he blinks, he's not dead yet.

Step 6: Check for gag reflex.

Jam a stick or a pen into the back of the alleged dead person's throat. If he's dead, he will not gag.

HOW TO SAVE SOMEONE WHO HAS FLAT-LINED

Henry Frankenstein (Colin Clive): *Look! It's moving. It's alive. It's alive . . .
It's alive, it's moving, it's alive, it's alive, it's alive, it's alive, IT'S ALIVE!*
    —*Frankenstein* (1931)

Bringing someone back from the dead is perhaps one of the most dramatic and emotionally satisfying skills an action hero can ever learn. There's nothing quite like that feeling of satisfaction you get when you successfully revive your key witness, your rowdy but lovable buddy cop, or that longtime unrequited love who just reentered your life. Yes, it goes without saying that successfully completing the near-death Hail Mary pass is a good skill to know—especially if you both plan to return for a sequel. Andrew J. Michaels, M.D., M.P.H., F.A.C.S. provides the essential info below.

Step 1: Check the patient to determine whether or not he's really dead.

If you are in a hospital, check the monitor to see if it has just slipped off your patient, which would result in a flat line. Look, listen, and feel for breathing and a pulse. Place your face near his mouth and watch his chest. If there is no activity, sound of breathing, or wind on your cheek, he's not breathing. (See "How to Tell When Someone Is Really Dead," p. 42.)

Step 2: Open the patient's airway.

Use one of the following techniques to obtain an airway:
- Place a small rolled-up towel or shirt underneath his shoulder blades to maintain this position while you work. Extend your patient's neck and use your index finger to clear your patient's mouth of any foreign objects.

- Roll the patient on his side with one leg flexed so that he is resting in the same manner in which he might be sleeping.

Warning: In a trauma situation you must be very careful of any potential neck injury. If neck injury is suspected, lift his jaw while keeping the neck in a neutral position.

Step 3: Inject a dose of epinephrine (adrenaline)—as much as 5 to 10 ccs of 1:10,000 or up to 5 ccs of 1:1000—into your patient's heart or trachea.

To inject into the trachea, find the hollow region about an inch below the Adam's apple. Inject the epinephrine just through the membrane at the midline of the hollow.

To inject it into the heart, find the notch below the ribs (beneath the sternum). Aim deep and toward the left nipple. Once the needle is in place, pull back on the plunger. If you get blood, you have found the heart—inject the epinephrine immediately.

If these techniques are unsuccessful, you may need to perform a tracheotomy to create an air passage (see p. 47).

Step 4: Begin CPR.

Note: The following process describes cardiopulmonary resuscitation for an adult only.

Place your hands at the lower edge of the sternum—located in the upper middle section of the chest. With one hand on top of the other, compress the chest about two inches with the heel of one hand. Compress the chest five times quickly, and have your partner (if you have one) breathe into the patient's trachea tube or mouth once. If you are alone, compress the chest fifteen times and breathe into the patient's airway once.

If you are in the E.R. and the chest is open, squeeze the heart directly using the same ratios as above.

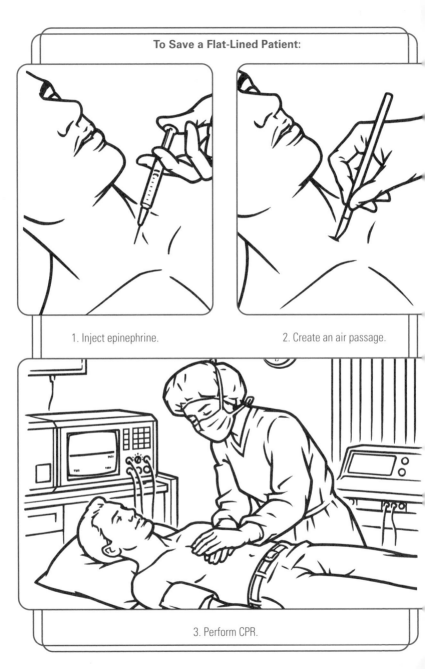

To Save a Flat-Lined Patient:

1. Inject epinephrine.

2. Create an air passage.

3. Perform CPR.

PERFORMING A TRACHEOTOMY

- Cut a hole in the hollow below the Adam's apple—where you injected the epinephrine.

- Make a vertical incision about one to two inches in length.

- Cut through the skin, through the soft tissue below, and then through the windpipe in the hollow. Try not to cut through the cartilage or the back wall of the trachea.

- Insert a hollow tube a couple centimeters in diameter into the center of the hole so the patient can have an air passage.

Continue until the patient is resuscitated—or until there is no chance of revival. Of course, depending on the situation—and how much you want the patient to live, dammit—you may not have a choice. If the patient is in a hypothermic state, suffering from electrical shock, or anything other than a hemorrhage, you may want to continue until you simply cannot go on.

Note: As long as you secure an airway within the first two to three minutes, your patient should have a fair chance of avoiding major brain damage. At more than six minutes, however, damage is bound to be severe.

HOW TO DRIVE A BUS AT HIGH SPEED

Howard Payne (Dennis Hopper): *Pop quiz, hot shot. There's a bomb on a bus. Once the bus hits fifty miles an hour, the bomb is armed. If the bus drops below fifty, it blows up. What do you do?*
—*Speed*

Driving a bus at a speed of 50 mph or higher is dangerous enough—whether or not you have a bomb onboard. You must keep your wits about you to protect your passengers, pedestrians, and third-party vehicles; so once you're behind the wheel, stay focused, and forget about the bomb and whatever else is going on in your life. Ask your fellow passengers for help when needed (especially the cute, perky ones with the bedroom eyes). And follow the advice here, from former Amalgamated Transit Union accident committee member and bus driver Bob Tyree.

Step 1: Alert the authorities.
Use your radio to call dispatch and tell them that you are on a freeway and will have to drive at least 50 mph. Ask for a police escort.

Step 2: Head for open, clear road.
If you are in the city, try to find a street with very little traffic and synchronized lights that will lead you to a highway or open road. Be aware of the other cars around you—most city drivers will not get out of the way or let buses into the flow of traffic. Be aware of drivers cutting you off, and watch out for pedestrians. Use your horn to warn people that you are coming and cannot stop for them.

Step 3: Move into a carpool lane.

If your city has one and traffic is low, move into the carpool lane.
Use your horn to move other cars out of the way. Most cities have
highway speeds of 65 mph, so as long as you don't hit traffic you
should be all right.

Step 4: Be careful on corners.

A bus is designed to take highway corners at posted speed limits,
but since you will have to be driving at 50 mph or higher, you'll
need to change your driving technique when going around corners. Start from as far outside as you can, then turn toward the
inside of the curve. Accelerate slightly through the corner and
move back to the outside as you come out of the turn.

Step 5: In case of a traffic slowdown on the highway, use the sideswipe ver-
sus head- or tail-on collision to move past the other cars.

If you have to collide with another vehicle, swipe the side of their
vehicle with yours. At all costs avoid head- or tail-on collisions.

Step 6: Steer to the right.

As a general rule, steering to the right is common practice for

---

PRE-TRIP BUS INSPECTION TIPS

- Check the condition of the tires, suspension, and windshield.

- Test the dashboard operations—horn, wipers, turn signals, lights, and door control.

- Make sure the steering wheel has less than two inches of play before the wheels
begin to turn.

- Once you've started the engine, inch the bus forward slowly and step on the brake
pedal to be sure that the brakes are functioning properly.

- Adjust your mirrors.

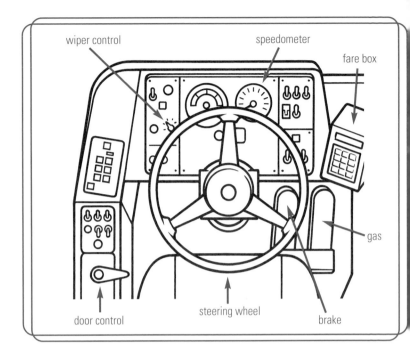

wiper control

speedometer

fare box

gas

door control

steering wheel

brake

avoiding head-on collisions. If collision is unavoidable, choose the lesser of two evils: hit a telephone pole instead of a pedestrian.

Step 7: To allow a bomb-squad technician to board the bus while you're still moving, open the door using the door control lever.

Match your speed to the squad car's and keep the doors aligned. Keep your eyes on the road as the technician comes on board.

Step 8: Once the situation is resolved, stop the bus.

Take your foot off the gas. If your brakes are still functioning, gradually step on the pedal until the bus fades to a stop. If your brakes fail to function properly, downshift into a lower gear and use the engine's natural braking ability.

HOW TO NEGOTIATE
A HOSTAGE CRISIS

Lt. Chris Sabian (Kevin Spacey): *You hurt one of them, you burn up any currency you have with me. They're all I care about. Getting you out of here alive . . . a distant second.*
  —The Negotiator

An action hero who is required to negotiate a hostage situation must remain calm above all else—"action," in fact, is the last resort in this situation. You must do everything you can to defuse the potentially lethal situation without the use of force. What you say or do not say can cost innocent victims their lives—so analyze your hostage taker, make him or her feel like you understand, and don't bring up any perceived inadequacies. Whatever the situation, your goal is the safety of the hostages. The information below comes directly from senior hostage negotiator Sgt. Larry J. Chavez, of the Sacramento Police Department.

Step 1: Evacuate the area.
  Minimize the threat of damage from a bomb or a wild bullet by evacuating the area within at least a full block of the building in which the hostages are being held. Across the street may seem far enough on a dog day afternoon, but it isn't, in reality. Tape off and control foot traffic and street traffic in the radius. You should have a team of security officers or authorities who can assist you.

Step 2: Have your team cover any and all potential points of entry and exit to the building.
  Cover doors, windows, ventilation shafts, and delivery bays.

Step 3: Gather as much intelligence information on your hostage taker as possible.

Find out who your hostage taker is. Does he have family and friends? Ask around at the scene for any witnesses who might know the hostage taker. Have a few members of your team interrogate witnesses in the area.

Find out what drove your hostage taker to this point. More often than not, a hostage taker will be in his present position due to a culmination of several unresolved issues. Know that your hostage taker may not be reacting to the facts, but rather to his perceptions of events, which may be darker than they really are. Be aware that if his loss is significant enough, he may be looking to exact revenge and then take his own life.

Step 4: Place yourself in the hostage taker's shoes and understand his burdens.

Understand that the hostage taker usually believes the police are there just to kill him. Why else would they be laying siege with their guns at the ready? He also usually believes that, regardless of the outcome, he will be in prison for life.

UNDERSTANDING THE HOSTAGE TAKER'S MIND

The hostage taker is burdened by the hostages he keeps. Despite popular perception, holding hostages takes a great deal of effort, since:

- **Maintaining vigilance is difficult.**
- **Some hostages may panic at the sight of a gun.**
- **Some hostages may react emotionally.**
- **Some hostages may attempt to escape.**
- **Some hostages may faint or have medical problems.**
- **Some hostages may challenge the hostage taker.**

These factors will make your negotiations even more difficult—so you must understand what you're up against.

Step 5: Locate the phone number of the building or space in which the hostage taker is holding his hostages.

Step 6: Call the number, and when the hostage taker picks up, ask if he is all right.

The hostage taker will most likely be caught off guard that you have not asked him to surrender immediately, so be prepared for an emotional answer to your first phone call. Remember, a hostage taker is under a lot of stress. Be sure to maintain composure and communicate in a nonthreatening manner.

Step 7: Ask if the "other people there" are all right.

Do not use the word "hostage"! This will just add to the hostage taker's stress.

Step 8: Assure the hostage taker that you are not there to hurt him, and try to gain his trust.

Tell him that if you were there to hurt him, you would have already done so. Practice "active listening" to help gain the hostage taker's trust:

- Carefully repeat back all of the information he has offered. The greater detail you can go into about his demands, the better. He wants a bus: How big? Metro or charter? Cigarettes? What brand? Filtered or nonfiltered? Light, ultralight, or regular? And on and on. This will buy you much-needed time as well as help tire him out.

- Encourage conversation. When there is a pause in the conversation, ask the hostage taker to continue to talk.

- Build a you-and-him-against-the-world relationship. When your hostage taker demands something, tell him that you have to negotiate with the scene commander. Always tell the hostage taker that anything you cannot do for him is the commander's responsibility. He will bond with you.

- Ask for a solution. By allowing the hostage taker to offer a solution, you create a potential win-win situation.

Step 9: **Negotiate for a solution by reassuring the hostage taker that you want to give him what he wants, but also let him know that you are in control.**

- Ask for a good-faith gesture in return for an immediate demand—continuing negotiations, proof of life, or even a hostage exchange.
- Don't be too specific about meeting his demands. If he asks for cigarettes, don't give him a whole pack (unless he asks for a full pack). Just give him a few. He'll be asking for more later. If he is angered by these limitations, blame the commander, and tell him you'll try to get him more—in exchange for another gesture on his part.

Step 10: **Once a trusting communication has been established, explain to the hostage taker that your talks will continue so long as no one is injured or assaulted.**

Tell him that, if anything happens to the hostages, you will no longer be able to help him, and the scene commander will turn responsibility over to the SWAT team to end the standoff.

Step 11: **If you hear shots and cannot confirm that anyone is injured, immediately ask for proof of life.**

Ask to talk to the hostages and confirm that they are all right. If you hear shots and confirm injury/death, the negotiations are over. Your team should enter the space and end the standoff.

HOW TO TAKE A BULLET

Frank Horrigan (Clint Eastwood): *I normally prefer not to get to know the people I'm protecting.*
Lilly Raines (Rene Russo): *Oh yeah? Why's that?*
Horrigan: *Well, you never know. You might decide they're not worth taking a bullet for.*
    —*In the Line of Fire*

The action hero faced with taking a bullet will have only a moment to react, and in that moment you must be prepared to give up your life. Remember, the assailant in the situation always has the upper hand—he knows what he's about to do. You do not. And so, you must be prepared. You must be resolute and focused. And you must protect yourself with body armor whenever possible—at the very least, with a bulletproof vest or a bible over your heart. Try to keep your head low, and use these steps, compliments of security specialist Shawn Engbrecht, to stay alert and alive.

Step 1: Stay as close as possible to the person you are protecting.
If you are working alone, stay just in front of and to one side of your defendee. If you are working with several other guards, surround the defendee's back and sides in addition to covering the front.

Step 2: Keep your eyes peeled for anything out of the ordinary.
If you are in a crowd of 30 people and 29 of them are smiling and cheering, keep your eyes on the one who is not smiling and cheering and is wearing the "People Suck" T-shirt.

Stand between shooter and target, face shooter, and place chest in line of fire.

Step 3: Watch the hands.

When an assailant pulls a gun, his hands make the first move.

Step 4: Position yourself between whomever you are protecting and the weapon.

Stand face front with respect to the shooter, with your arms extended out to your sides to make the shooter's target more difficult to hit. If you have time, push your defendee to the ground before assuming this position.

Step 5: Attempt to place your chest in the line of fire (remember, you'll be wearing a bulletproof vest).

If the shooter is using a rifle from a distance, you probably won't see him coming—or be able to stop the bullet. Your body armor will protect your chest from a relatively close-range bullet. Estimate the target line of the bullet by watching the barrel of the gun.

Step 6: If you cannot put your chest in the line of fire, put your arm, leg, or shoulder in the line of fire.

Reach toward the target line with an arm, step toward the target line with a leg, or turn into the target line with a shoulder.

Step 7: Take the hit.

Most body armor will resist a handgun bullet shot at close range. However, the force from the weapon may knock you back, so stand your ground. If you have time, set your weight onto your back foot and step forward into the bullet with your opposite foot.

HOW TO DODGE THE SHOT

Once your defendee is in a secure location—a car, building, or other safe haven—you may need to dodge the bullets rather than intercept them. Use the following methods:

- **Blade your body toward the gun.**
Turn your body so that it is as narrow as possible when facing the gun. Keep your arms snug against your body.

- **Run in a zigzag pattern away from the gunfire.**
Choose a course with the shortest distance to cover—toward a building, car, and so forth. This "haphazard" zigzag movement will make you harder to target.

HOW TO SAVE SOMEONE FROM BEING HIT BY A SPEEDING CAR

Dr. Steve Edison (Matthew McConaughey) (out of breath and on the ground on top of Mary): *You okay?*
Mary Fiore (Jennifer Lopez): *You saved my shoe . . . I . . . mmm . . . my life.*
—*The Wedding Planner*

When walking on or near the street, the action hero should stay particularly alert and aware—hit-and-run attempts always have a way of finding the action hero. Be especially aware around members of the witness-protection program, secret agents, and wedding planners in stiletto heels. Once you have saved yourself (and anyone else), seek medical attention immediately, even if you both feel OK. This will ensure no permanent damage was done, and give you much-needed time to fall in love during Act II. Here's how stuntman Christopher Caso advises the hero to make his move.

Step 1: Try to warn the person that a car is coming.

Call out or yell to the potential victim that a car is coming and she is about to be hit. If she does not hear you or there is no time to yell, you will need to act.

Step 2: Start running toward the potential victim.

Humans have the ability to do lightning-fast calculations in their heads during times of danger—for example, determining how fast you have to move to save the person. The problem is getting your body to agree with your mind. Do not hesitate—start running immediately.

Tackle your subject to remove her from harm's way.

Jump, tuck, and roll to safety over a small car.

Center body and lie flat until the semi passes over.

Step 3: As you run, try to get a sense of how long it will be before your victim is hit.

Will you be able to reach her in time to shout a warning for her to move, or will you have to tackle or shove her out of the way?

Step 4: Keep shouting "look out" or "get out of the way" as you run.

As you come closer to your subject, she may be able to hear you better.

Step 5: Tackle your subject to remove her from harm's way.

Dive at the person as if you were making a football tackle. Your body weight and momentum should be enough to move her out of the way.

Step 6: Wrap your arms around your subject's head and upper body as you tackle her.

Try to keep those vital areas protected.

Step 7: Hit the ground rolling like a log.

Once you've tackled the victim, continue to hold her to your side. As you approach the ground, roll your weight onto the shoulder that's farthest from the car's path. Continue to roll over and over again, until you are entirely clear of the car.

Step 8: Immediately get out of the street.

Just because you've gotten out of one car's path doesn't mean another one isn't barreling toward you in the opposite lane.

HOW TO SAVE YOURSELF

When you alone are the person in danger of being hit by an oncoming car or truck, you must make some split-second decisions based on the type of vehicle heading toward you.

SMALL CARS

- **If you are being approached by a small car or one with a low profile, face the car and jump as high as possible at the last possible moment. The goal is to jump up and over the car as it passes by.**

- **As you roll up over the car, tuck yourself into a ball.**
This way if a foot or leg gets hit by the car, you will "spin" over it rather than being tossed up into the air.

SEMI TRUCKS

- **If you are being approached by a semi with about two feet of ground clearance, hit the ground.**
With your feet facing the truck, center yourself between its wheels. Lie as flat as you can and protect your face.

- **Keep all body parts squeezed to the ground as the truck passes over you.**
Do not raise your head or arms as the truck passes. There are usually about twelve inches of clearance beneath a standard 18-wheeler, so as long as the truck isn't dragging anything, you should be OK. Just watch for low-riding differentials.

- **If there is not enough ground clearance beneath the truck, hit the ground and roll out of the way (see step 7).**

Sarah (Michelle Joyner): *Help! Hal, I'm slipping!*
Hal (Michael Rooker): *Gabe, man—don't you lose her! Don't you let her go!*
Sarah: *Don't let me fall . . . I'm slipping! Haaal!*
Gabe (Sylvester Stallone): *Sarah please . . .*
Sarah: *No. No! I'm slipping. Gabe! Gabe, don't let me fall! No. Help me—*
   I'm falling! (She falls.) *Gaaaaaaaaaaaaabbbbbbbe!*
         —Cliffhanger

Don't let this happen to you. The accomplished action hero is one who knows how to save someone hanging by a finger from the edge of a cliff. You must move quickly: unless the dangler is anchored to secure ground, you have only a few minutes to pull him or her to safety. If you don't succeed, you may find you have let yourself or a close personal friend and climbing partner down (way down). The information here comes from stuntman and gymnast Christopher Caso.

IF THE VICTIM IS
WITHIN YOUR REACH

Step 1: Find solid footing near where the victim is hanging.
   Stand on a surface that you are sure *will not* budge—a large boulder, a firm ledge, or a live tree. If you are not safe, you may both wind up at the bottom of the cliff.

Step 2: Help the victim stay calm.
   Whoever is hanging must stay calm to conserve as much energy as possible. Reassure him that he will be all right, but that he needs

to hold very still. Tell him to stay calm and relaxed. Tell him panic is not an option. Try to keep him focused on the solution rather than the problem. No matter how you are able to help him up, you will need his strength to assist you.

Step 3: Dry your hands.

If you have climber's chalk, use it to dry your hands. Otherwise, use some dry dirt or just wipe your hand on your pants. This is no time for clammy hands.

Step 4: If you have solid footing, use both hands to clasp at least one of the victim's hands.

Otherwise, hold on to a tree or rock with one hand and clasp his hand with the other.

Step 5: If you cannot reach his hand, grab anything he is wearing.

If you are looking at a life-or-death situation, just grab anything you can to get a solid grip—a coat, a harness, even his hair will suffice if it's long enough. In the heat of the moment, there's not much time to choose what to grab. But be careful when grabbing clothes—they may be loose and slip off or tear.

Step 6: Pull him to safety.

Pulling a 180-pound person from a dead hang takes some serious strength. However, in such extreme circumstances you will most likely have a solid dose of adrenaline pumping through your veins to help you out. If possible, have the victim climb as you pull.

IF THE VICTIM IS
OUT OF ARM'S REACH

Rescue with a Branch

As above, find some solid footing for yourself and remind the victim to stay calm and retain his energy.

Step 1: Find a solid branch.

The thinner the better—so he can get a solid grip. But the branch better be a very hard, dense wood. If you can, find a branch that has a little live bark or extra branches on it for grip.

Step 2: Lower the branch to him.

Lower the branch far enough that he can get a solid grasp on it.

Step 3: Hold the branch firmly or pull him to safety.

From solid ground, hold the branch so he can climb up. Alternatively, if you have the strength, you may help to pull him up by pulling the branch toward you.

Rescue with a Rope

As above, find some solid footing for yourself and remind the victim to stay calm and retain his energy.

Step 1: Tie the rope to a rock or tree that is solidly anchored into the ground.

Use a figure-eight knot around the rock or tree. Quickly test it a few times after you have tied it off. Wind the end of the rope around the tree or rock once or twice. Leave just enough rope so that you still have enough length to lower to the victim, but not so much that there is too much slack.

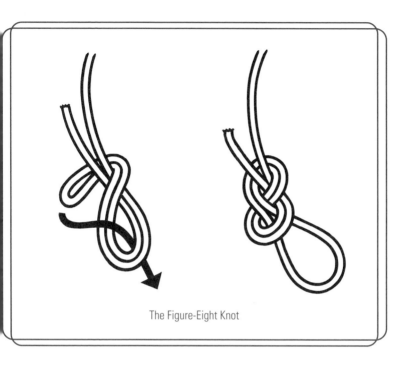

The Figure-Eight Knot

Step 2: Loop and tie the other end of the rope.

Using a figure-eight knot, tie the other end of the rope into a "stirrup"-sized loop (large enough to fit a foot).

Step 3: Lower the rope to the victim and pull him up.

If the victim can step into the loop, tighten the rope so that he has the leverage to get a better handhold on the ground and pull himself up. If he cannot step into the loop, have him grab the rope and use your own leverage to pull him up toward the tree or rock.

CHAPTER 2
Love Skills

DON'T BELIEVE WHAT YOU SEE in the movies and on television—money and power don't really make the world go 'round. It's love that motivates us all. You think those evil geniuses would be so hell-bent on ruling the world if they had been brought up in loving families, or if they had a good man or woman to keep them company? Of course not—evil geniuses don't want to be evil. They just want to be loved.

Lovemaking skills are essential to the success of every action hero—not just British secret agents with licenses to kill. After all, without love skills, the romantic action hero has no other means of relieving the tension—aside from a good fight. Without love skills, the action hero has no one to share the joys of victory with—or to commiserate with in defeat. Without love skills, the action hero is always on the run, looking for more, well, action. But with the skills in this section, you'll learn to enjoy your action hero's lifestyle and live life to the fullest—to pick someone up in a bar or seduce an attractive but stubborn colleague. So go ahead—stop a wedding. Seduce an enemy agent. Mix a love potion. Heck, fall in love with a replicant. Live a little. Love a little.

HOW TO STOP A WEDDING

Benjamin Braddock (Dustin Hoffman) (banging on church window):
Elaine! Elaine! Elaine!
    —*The Graduate*

As a general rule, if you are going to try to stop a wedding, you should attempt do so well before the "speak now or forever hold your peace" part. Emotions will be running high at the event—even if you haven't been having an affair with the bride's alcoholic mother—so you need to be prepared. For a ceremonial interruption, you should have your words ready (know what you're going to say to the bride or groom, the jilted lover, and the guests). Above all, have an escape route planned—or at least get familiar with the local bus schedule. The information here comes from expert wedding consultant Sara L. Ambarian.

Warning: Just because you are enough in love with someone to stop your beloved's wedding and profess your feelings does not mean he or she feels the same way. You may be walking out the door alone—so you need to prepare yourself for that possibility as well.

Step 1: Find out where the wedding will be held.
   If you speak to family or friends of the bride and groom, be subtle. Don't let on that you are planning to stop the wedding. If you cannot get the information from family and friends, then look in the newspapers. Often, upcoming wedding announcements will appear in the Weddings section. You can also call or visit likely churches or reception halls where the wedding might be held.

Step 2: Pick the spot from which you will speak.

Be sure to pick a spot that offers both dramatic effect *and* safety. A balcony in a church has the effect of being dramatic, but perhaps not the security of a solid escape route—if things take a turn for the worse. If you stand at the rear of the main aisle, you can get your point across and have quick access to the front door if you need to make a quick escape.

Step 3: Determine what you will say.

If you have the ability for clear and passionate self-expression under high pressure, then trust yourself and speak from your heart. If your talents lie elsewhere, then write your feelings down on index cards beforehand. Do not, however, rely on speaking from the cards during your "break-in." Practice. Be sure to say what you need to say from the heart and from memory. (Index cards do not exactly say "true love.")

Step 4: Wait until the officiant says "speak now" to speak now.

Timing is everything. If you have done everything you can to speak your mind before the ceremony, you should now wait your turn to speak. Appropriately timing your speech will make your plea seem more imperative. Remember: The closer you get to the moment when the bride and groom speak their vows, the more emotionally charged everyone involved will be—so be prepared for verbal or physical confrontations (see "Other Wedding-Busting Tips," p. 70).

Step 5: State your case effectively.

Tell the bride or groom:

- He or she cannot marry [INSERT NAME].
- Why he or she cannot marry [INSERT NAME AND REASON].
- How much you love him or her.

OTHER WEDDING-BUSTING TIPS

■ **Be aware of the financial and emotional cost of a cancelled wedding.**
The families and couples involved will most certainly be upset by your interruption. Acknowledge this in your speech. This may also help to defuse any verbal confrontations.

■ **Do everything in your power to defuse a volatile situation.**
If someone is threatening you, don't be aggressive. Just make your plea without provoking anyone more than you already have. Use a head-down, subservient posture to show that you're a lover not a fighter.

■ **Offer to pay any bills.**
If you are successful in stopping your love's wedding, and you can spare the cash, offer to pay the bills for the wedding. It may be expensive, but it's a small price to pay to gain favor.

■ **If you are unsuccessful in stopping the wedding and you are rejected, do your best to leave quietly.**
Be apologetic, self-effacing, and nonconfrontational. Simply and quietly back your way out of the room.

Step 6: Have a good escape route.

You do not necessarily have to leave the wedding hand-in-hand with your love. In fact, you may be safer leaving alone and contacting each other when everyone has cooled down a bit.

However, if everything goes well and your love runs down the aisle or up to the balcony to be with you, be prepared. Try to have a car and driver waiting near your exit. If that is not possible, determine the nearest subway or bus stop location, or pay a taxi to wait outside the ceremony. Steal the "Just Married" car only as a last resort—true love is admirable, but grand theft auto is not.

HOW TO DIRTY DANCE

Johnny Castle (Patrick Swayze): ***No one puts Baby in a corner.***
    —*Dirty Dancing*

It's handy to know how to shake your action hero booty on the dance floor. A strong knowledge of dance moves—particularly the various forms of dirty dancing—is invaluable when it comes to seducing an enemy agent, blending in at a party, or saving the day at a summer resort. Dancing is a great way to blend into the crowd, to strut your stuff, and of course—when done properly—to have the time of your life. To that end, we offer the following directions, provided by theater choreographer Cynthia Fleming.

WARMING UP

The Dirty Dance is all in the hips. Practice these hip warmups standing side-by-side with your partner. Use the music you'll be dancing to when you perform.

- Stand with your back straight and your knees slightly bent.
- Put your hands on your hips.
- Moving together, push your hips forward and back. Do several reps of this move. The goal here is to get used to isolating the hip movement. It may help to call out, "forward-and-back" as you move forward and back.
- Moving together, push your hips right, then left. Do several reps of this move.
- Moving together, push your hips in circles. Do several reps. You can call out, "forward-and-right-and-back-and-left." Practice moving both clockwise and counterclockwise.

DANCING GLOSSARY

"Footloose"—To dance out your anger alone in various warehouses and roller mills. Moves may include sliding down stair rails or flailing wildly down narrow aisles of steel storage rooms.

"Flashdance"—To dance freestyle in the face of modern-day ballet conventions. Moves may include splashing yourself with a bucket of water or running madly in place.

"Dirty Dance"—To dance as if you are having sex standing up, with your clothes on. Find a dance partner with whom you are comfortable and practice in your home before going out in public.

THE MOVES

The following moves are described from the leader's perspective. Some basic pointers:

- Hold your partner's right hand at about shoulder height with your left hand. Your right hand should be on her left shoulder blade—but flexible enough to move up and down her back.
- Her left hand should be on your right shoulder.
- Combine the moves in any order you see fit.
- "Groove" with the music and build the dance as the music builds.

Move A: The Basic Grind

Step 1: As above, put your hands in position.

Stand facing each other with your feet about shoulder width apart.

Step 2: Step forward—connecting at the hips—so that your partner's thigh is between your legs.

Hold your hips tightly together, but stay loose up top and fluid on your feet.

Step 3: Move your hips together in any of the various directions (as in the warmup).

Lead strongly—force your partner to follow. This is the staple Dirty Dancing position and movement. Begin here and return here when venturing into any of the following combinations.

Move B: The Flamingo

From the Basic Grind position, the Flamingo is as follows.

Step 1: Your partner—while still connected to you at the hands and hips—moves her torso to your right.

Step 2: Simultaneously, she turns her head and looks out (so that she is looking in the same direction as you are), brings her right knee up to about waist level, and holds it against your waist.

Step 3: She holds this position for a moment and then resumes the Basic Grind position.

Move C: The Dip

From the Basic Grind, move your partner into the Dip in one of the following manners:

Method A: Place your right hand on your partner's left shoulder blade. With your left hand, push her to your right side and back so that she arches her back and dips down to your right. Keep your hips closely connected at all times.

Method B: Place your right hand on your partner's waist (left side). Dip her backward so that her back arches and her head drops back. As above, keep your hips connected throughout.

Dirty Dancing Moves

The Basic Grind

The Dip

The Flamingo

The Spin

The Jump

Move D: The Spin

Step 1: From the Basic Grind, place your right hand on your partner's waist (left side).

Step 2: With your right hand, push her waist away, while your left hand pulls her around.

She spins until you pull her back in and resume the Basic Grind. Conversely, you can push with your left hand and pull with your right hand to spin her in the other direction.

Move E: The Jump

Warning: The Jump is a very complicated move to hold. If you are not professional dancers but insist on trying it, set up some mattresses or another soft landing surface beforehand.

Step 1: Stand at one end of the room, with your feet firmly planted and knees slightly bent. Your partner should be at the other end of the room.

Step 2: Your partner should run up to you, put her hands on your shoulders, and jump and push up simultaneously.

Step 3: When she approaches, pick her up with both hands from her waist.

Step 4: Straighten your legs and lift her up over your head.

She should stiffen her body and hold position. When done correctly, the partners' positions should form a "T."

Lovelorn Lady (Anabella Price): *I want him to want me so much that he can't stand it.*
Aunt Bridget "Jet" Owens (Dianne Wiest): *Be careful what you wish for.*
    —*Practical Magic*

Most action heroes with any amount of lovemaking ability will not need to use love potions to pitch their woo. However, when time is of the essence, the love potion can be a helpful tool. Love potions—or *philters*, as they are sometimes called—were once made with such ingredients as human blood, urine, and sexual secretions. Today, love potions are more subtle. Magical potions, made with care and flower petals by practicing witches, can be very effective tools to sway an allegiance—or just make life a little more interesting. These instructions (and a recipe) come by way of witch, astrologer, and minister Gerina Dunwich.

LOVE POTION BUILT FOR TWO

What You'll Need
- Fresh, unopened magnolia buds (one handful)
- Rainwater (two cups)
- Honey (one tablespoon)
- A small pot or cauldron

Step 1: Pick the right moment to prepare your potion.

To work properly, a love potion must be prepared at the right times. Follow these simple rules:

- Prepare during a waxing lunar phase for attracting.
- Prepare during a waning lunar phase for repelling.
- For greater effectiveness, brew on a Friday (the day of the week ruled by the love goddess Venus).
- For even greater effectiveness, brew on Valentine's Day (February 14) or St. Agnes's Eve (January 20). These are traditional times for preparing love potions, according to witches and practitioners of European folk magic.

Step 2: Charm your ingredients.

Charge your ingredients with magical energy by concentrating on the desired outcome of your spell. Use an incantation you are comfortable with. Write your own or recite the following:

Herbs of Venus, work for me.
This is my will. So mote it be.

Step 3: Prepare your potion.

Place the unopened magnolia buds and two cups of rainwater into a small pot or cauldron. Brew for twenty minutes, uncovered. Stir occasionally; while brewing, concentrate deeply on the person whose affections you desire. Remove from heat and let cool. Strain and sweeten with a tablespoon of honey. Makes one serving.

Proper use of a love potion can hasten a seduction or sway an allegiance.

Step 4: Raise, direct, and release the potion's magical energy.

Use an incantation to increase the magical energy around your spell. Chant or dance your own energy-raising rite or recite the following:

Let the one who drinks this potion
Shower me with love's emotion.

Step 5: Pick the correct time to serve your potion.

Be sure that your potion is ingested on the proper lunar schedule for the desired result: waxing lunar phase for attracting, waning lunar phase for repelling.

Step 6: Add the potion to the food or drink of the person you desire, and serve.

Effects depend on the person's metabolism, but should be rather sudden. Have faith in yourself and your powers—the more you believe in yourself and your powers of enchantment, the more effective your potion will be.

BREAKING A LOVE SPELL

Undoing the spell of a love potion can sometimes be tricky. Should you need to reverse a spell, attempt one of the following methods:

- **Repeat the steps of the original spell in reverse during a waning moon. Recite any incantations backward. Make the potion again by adding the ingredients in reverse order.**

- **Carry a white silk charm bag filled with angelica leaves. Angelica leaves, found in specialty herb shops, are used to protect from evil and for exorcisms.**

- **Drink the juice from a vervain plant gathered before sunrise. Vervain plants, also found in herb shops, are used in reverse love spells.**

- **Criticize, argue, or break up with the person who is under your spell. It isn't magic, but it works.**

Ned Racine (William Hurt): *Me, I need tending. Someone to take care of me. Someone to rub my tired muscles, smooth out my sheets.*
Matty Walker (Kathleen Turner): *Get married.*
Ned: *I just need it for tonight.*
　　　—Body Heat

Picking someone up in a bar has many advantages (besides the obvious ones). Barfly companions can be of great assistance in your adventures—they can treat your wounds and help you escape pursuers, provide important information, give you a place to crash for the night, and may even end up joining you in your quest (or for the rest of your life). When attempting a bar pickup, rely on these simple rules: be yourself, be suave, do not act desperate, and don't order any drinks with umbrellas in them. These instructions are brought to you by longtime bartender Craig Lowe.

Step 1: Scout the room.

Choose a spot in the bar where you can observe the entire space. Casually glance around until you see a person you would like to pick up.

THINGS YOU SHOULD NOT SAY

- Are you from Tennessee? 'Cause you're the only 10 I see.

- What has two thumbs and likes you? Me!

- Would you like to have breakfast? Should I call or just nudge?

- Are those real?

Step 2: Move in closer.

Find a spot within that person's line of sight, but not directly so. You should be to one side or the other.

Step 3: Make initial eye contact.

Casually catch the eye of the person you would like to pick up. DO NOT STARE! (Staring may come across as scary rather than attractive.) Just glance long enough to see whether or not this person might be interested in you. If you get a good "vibe," smile briefly and look away.

Step 4: Buy him a drink.

Ask the bartender or waiter to give the person whatever they would like. DO NOT SEND OVER A DRINK OF YOUR CHOOSING. Let the person choose the drink.

Step 5: Make eye contact again when the drink is offered and then delivered.

Do not approach him yet—simply watch as the bartender delivers your offer and then the drink. Make eye contact again and see if your target responds positively. This can be a bit tricky at times. If there is little or no eye contact, this doesn't mean you are out of the game—but it isn't too promising. Above all, pay attention to body language. If it seems he is open to conversation or gives you another smile, by all means continue the chase.

Step 6: Move quickly if you get a positive response.

Don't act desperate—but don't let too much time pass before going over. Behave as if you are just out to meet new people, have a good time, and make some friends. Smooth lines are unnecessary—a simple introduction will suffice at this point.

Step 7: Be yourself.

Try not to speak too loudly or arrogantly. Just be natural. If you're funny, be funny. If you're serious, be serious. Take an interest in this person's life, but don't get too personal right off the bat.

Step 8: Close the deal.

Ask confidently, but not arrogantly, for what you want and you will likely get it, whether you want a companion for the night, for the rest of the adventure, or for the rest of your life.

HOW TO TURN SEXUAL TENSION INTO MAD, PASSIONATE SEX

Sam Malone (Ted Danson): *You've made my life a living hell.*
Diane Chambers (Shelley Long): *I didn't want you to think I was easy.*
        —Cheers

A true action hero must know how to take the natural tension that exists in any adventure and turn it into something more passionate. Two people thrown together in dire circumstances already have a pretty good chance of hooking up—in the face of adversity, sexual tensions run rampant. However, in order to move things to the next level, you need to recognize the signs, signals, and opportunities that present themselves along the way. So make your move only after you have reached the safe house, the shower, or the Motel 6, and follow these instructions, from sexpert Carol Queen.

Step 1: Recognize the signs of sexual tension.

Look for the following signs of sexual tensions both in your potential partner and yourself:

- Fast or deep breathing
- Flushed cheeks, neck, and upper chest
- Dilated eyes
- Genital arousal
- Close talking
- Arguing

Any or all of the above symptoms may be indications that sexual tension is present. But be careful. People may show interest without necessarily being interested in another person sexually. Others may be too shy to make any other moves.

Step 2: Pick your moment.

Good moments to explore these tensions are:

- When your lives are in danger—but not immediately so.
- When you are locked together in a car trunk, trapped in an elevator, or in another confined space.
- When you are crashing in a motel room for the night while on the run.

Step 3: Begin to heighten the sexual tension slowly.

Proceed with caution. People who are truly sexually attracted to one another will use more eye contact than those who are just being social. People who are truly sexually attracted to one another tend to seek ways to increase intimacy, such as moving into each other's space.

Find opportunities to touch your potential partner. Beginning with less intimate areas, casually find ways to touch shoulders or arms.

Step 4: Create an opportunity to talk.

Depending upon the type of tension, this can either be an unexpected personal confession ("My first wife was killed five years ago") or a contrived argument to spur a reaction ("You're the most stubborn man I've ever known").

How this person responds (and whether he or she responds at all) will tell you how the tension is going to culminate. If your potential partner engages you in a passionate discussion or argument, you are on your way to that magic place. If not, back off immediately.

Step 5: Begin heavy flirting.

Once a true tension has been established and confirmed, proceed to engage in sexual banter and innuendo. Be subtle yet suggestive.

Recognize the signs of sexual tension . . .

fast breathing

flushed cheeks

close talking

. . . then pick your moment and make your move.

SEXUAL BANTER AND INNUENDO

Use any of the following techniques to engage in sexual banter and innuendo:

- **Be honest.**
Speak from the heart—or even a little lower down if that's where your passions lie.

- **Call attention to your potential partner's attractive temperament. Some sample lines:**
  - "Are you *always* this lively?"
  - "You're a real spitfire aren't you?"
  - "I can't believe you just fought off three henchmen without breaking a sweat!"

- **Flirt with your potential partner in-the-moment and make admiring remarks about his or her physical charms.**
  - Comment on his or her hair, clothes, body, or style.
  - Pick up on something suggestive he or she just said.
  - Avoid using old pickup or flirtation lines.

Step 6: **Examine your potential partner's body when you can do so without being too overt.**

Casually look over your potential partner's body with pleasure. Be careful here—you don't want to stare at body parts too long or else you risk crossing the line and becoming a pervert. Casual glances are more sexy than staring. Try to watch your potential partner's mouth as he or she speaks before glancing to the chest or groin.

Step 7: **Find the moment to make your move.**

Watch for the following signs before you make your move:

- Unbroken eye contact—move in for the kiss.
- Reciprocated touches in more intimate locations such as hands, knees, or thighs—move in for the hug/cuddle.

- A pregnant pause during a heightened argument—move in for the kiss.
- A final moment of quiet before a threatened execution, world takeover, or sting operation—move in for the nothing-to-lose, mad, passionate sex.

HOW TO KISS

As a general rule you should start small and slowly work up to the bigger, more intense kisses. If you initiate a kiss that your partner doesn't like, back off for a moment and then slowly begin again. Use any of the following techniques:

- **Soft, close-lipped kisses on the neck or sides of face.**

- **Moistened close-lipped kisses on the lips.**

- **Moistened, partly open-lipped kisses on the lips (no tongue).**

- **Open-mouthed kisses with tongue. As you move into this kiss, you may experience a wetter, harder kiss. Check in with your partner before moving on to the advanced tongue techniques, which include:**
  - Tongue between inner lips and gums.
  - Tongue thrusting forcefully into mouth.
  - Biting lips or tongue.

CHAPTER 3
Paranormal Skills

EVERY GOOD ACTION HERO knows to expect the unexpected—and even the unexplained. In the action hero's world, the extraordinary often happens: a parasite suddenly attaches itself to your face and impregnates you with a baby alien, you wander into a haunted house with bleeding walls, you encounter an Imperial guard who needs a little extra convincing. The well-rounded action hero isn't fazed by such things, because he or she is well versed in paranormal skills of all kinds. An action hero will fearlessly communicate with an alien—even the unfriendly ones who don't have glowing fingers and say, "Owwwwch." An action hero has the ability to see dead people, and, if necessary, can help them realize that they too are dead. An action hero can purge a home filled with ghosts.

Within this chapter, you will learn to become the best paranormal action hero you can be. You will learn such feats as the Jedi Mind Trick, the Vulcan Nerve Pinch, and even feats of clairvoyance—skills that defuse potentially lethal confrontations before they have a chance to happen.

Never again will you be at a loss when your daughter reaches up to the TV static and says, "They're here . . ." Read on, and remember—anything is possible in the action hero's world. Be ready.

HOW TO COMMUNICATE WITH AN EXTRATERRESTRIAL

E.T: *E.T. phone home.*
　　　—E.T.: The Extra-Terrestrial

When extraterrestrials arrive on earth they will most likely be of higher intelligence—even if they are not as good-looking as we are and don't speak our language. Therefore, you must assume that any E.T. who comes to earth is more advanced than you. (If you were more advanced, you would be the one visiting the E.T.) Many of your initial communication problems may be solved by the E.T.'s advanced technology. However, if this fails, and your Devil's Tower lightboard malfunctions, you need to establish some common ground for communication. Here is your communication guide, from John Elliott, B.Sc., M.Sc., Ph.D.

GENERAL GUIDELINES

- **Meet the E.T. with "openness."**
Much in the same way you would let a wild animal know that you mean it no harm, open your hands and arms to the E.T. This will show that you are offering your respect and trust. Assume—and hope—that the E.T. will greet you in a similar manner.

- **Try to stay calm.**
E.T.s can sense fear and may reflect your feelings right back with fear sensations of their own. Fear may also make them angry—and you wouldn't like them when they're angry.

- **Make "friendly" eye contact.**
Turning your head down or not making eye contact may imply subservience. Greet your E.T. with friendly eye contact, the way you might greet an old friend you haven't seen in a long time.

ESTABLISH A PRIMER

Consider your communications with an E.T. to be similar to those you would have with a Neanderthal. The only difference is that to the E.T., *you* are the Neanderthal. You must establish a common "language" within a common frame of reference.

Step 1: Establish the objects of reference.

Begin building a frame of reference by drawing two shapes. Include the name of the shape next to a picture of the shape itself.

Step 2: Establish the mathematics.

Use simple mathematics to portray the relations between your shapes through numbers. One ball is "one." Two balls are "two." Three balls are "three."

Step 3: Establish relationships among your numbers and shapes.

Put your shapes and numbers in relation to one another to show how "things" in your world interact.

Ball "on" box.   Balls "in" box.

"Where is your spaceship?"

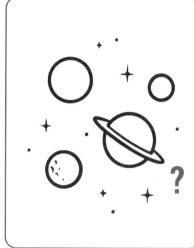

"Where are you from?"

"Please do not use me
for medical experiments."

"Welcome."

Step 4: Establish an elementary description of your world by naming objects.
As if you were teaching a child to speak or an adult a second language, begin to name your outside world. Show the E.T. a tree. Say "tree." Show the E.T. a rock. Say "rock." Show the E.T. colors and actions, and name each one in turn.

Step 5: Establish a description of your language.
Begin to describe, by example, prepositions, pronouns, and conjunctions. Use pictures or direct examples to portray your meanings. Point to yourself and say your name. Point to a man and say "he." Point to a woman and say "she." Point to both and say they. And so on. Display your words in relation to each other as you did with the objects in step 3, above.

Step 6: Establish your similarities with the E.T.
Using the primer, build on the similarities between you and the E.T. Evolution dictates some universal attributes for all advanced civilizations; for example, two or more eyes for depth perception, manipulators for dexterous work, reproductive systems for procreation, and so forth. Put your similarities into relation with the E.T.'s. Point to your eyes, then point to the E.T.'s eyes; point to your hands, then point to the E.T.'s hands; and so forth.

Step 7: Enjoy your conversation.
Once your primer has been established, the E.T. will most likely have a lot to tell you. Try to enjoy the conversation and don't let panic take over. This is your big chance to learn about life beyond the known universe.

HOW TO CONTACT THE DEAD

Cole Sear (Haley Joel Osment): *I see dead people.*
    —The Sixth Sense

For action heroes who don't have the natural ability to identify and converse with the dead, take heart: there are methods you can learn. Many mediums think that we're all able to sense the presence of the dead. You know those cold pricklies you get on your neck? Those vivid dreams you have of digging up the basement floor? That eerie reflection you see in the bathtub water? These aren't hallucinations or signs of illness—they're signs a dead person is present. The steps below have been provided by Tracey, an expert in the medium and divination arts.

Anyone can join you in a séance as long as they are committed to the success of the process. If you choose to work in a group of people, select participants who may want to contact someone of their own. You can attempt to contact anyone who has passed (though you may not always be successful).

Step 1: Choose a space and set the mood.

A quiet place is the only necessary element for holding a séance.

If you choose to have an indoor séance, smaller rooms tend to be more effective. They make it easier to know when the dead have arrived (see "How to Know When You See Dead People," p. 98). Turn down the lights, pull any curtains closed, and light a candle and place it in the middle of the room. You may use a table or sit on the floor.

If you choose to have an outdoor séance, pick a space that you can control access to and that has a general sense of "peace." A park is fine if you are surrounded by trees or bushes. You may light a candle if you are so inclined, though the natural element of the outdoors may prove to be sufficient to set the proper mood.

Note: One can contact the dead at any time of day, but if you are contacting the dead outside, nighttime or evening séances have been found to be most effective.

Step 2: As the leader of the séance, direct everyone in your group to hold hands.

This allows you to unite your energies and work as one. Direct everyone to tap into the group energy and work together.

Step 3: Take yourselves "down."

Using one of the following methods, each of the participants should take themselves to a place of sharpened focus.

- Meditation: Focus your eyes on the candle or an object in the center of your circle. Breathe in through the nose, hold the breath for three seconds, and then breathe out through the mouth for several long breaths (as long as it takes for you to feel that you or your group is focused on the task at hand).
- Prayer: Use whatever form of prayer your beliefs dictate to focus your energies in the room.

Step 4: Open a portal.

Direct the group to recite the following incantation:

This is a day that is not a day,
And a time that is not a time,
And a place that is not a place.
We want to open a portal between the worlds.

If you choose to ask in your own way, compose an incantation of your own. Be specific about asking for a portal to be opened between the worlds.

Step 5: Look for the ghosts.

When the spirits arrive you and the other participants may feel physical pressure, a chill, or actually hear and see them (see "How to Know When You See Dead People," p. 98). Not everyone has to feel the presence for it to be there. Some participants may be more sensitive than others.

To hold an indoor séance use a small, quiet room, turn down the lights, light a candle, hold hands, and take yourselves "down."

Step 6: Act natural when the spirits arrive.

The saying goes, "As above, so below." Spirits are generally the same in the spirit world as they were in the physical world. Both you and your participants should act naturally with them and they will respond in kind. Above all, be polite. Remember to say "please" and "thank you."

Step 7: Call the name of the spirit with whom you wish to speak.

Once you have opened a portal, any number of spirits may arrive at your séance. They can pass the word to whomever it is you would like to speak with. Call the name of the spirit and wait. It may take up to five minutes for the spirit to arrive. If five minutes have passed and your spirit has not arrived, the spirit is probably not coming.

Step 8: Try to connect with the spirit.

Use strategies to reconnect with a familiar spirit. If the two of you had a favorite song, request that you sing it together. If you have questions about the spirit's present or past memories, ask for the answers. Be aware, however, that the spirit won't know the answers to every question.

Step 9: When you are all satisfied with your session, close the portal.

Give the others the opportunity to speak to the spirits present, then thank the spirits who came to your séance and ask in your own way for the portal to be closed. You should be able to sense when all of the spirits have left and the portal is closed. If a spirit remains after the portal has closed, use the techniques described in "Warnings and Defenses" (p. 98) to remove them.

Step 10: Break hands with your group and open the circle.

WARNINGS AND DEFENSES

You might run into a spirit who was not so nice when he or she was still among the living. If you happen to contact one who seems mean or makes you uncomfortable, try these techniques to get the spirit to leave.

▪ Stay strong.
Remember that spirits only have as much power over you as you allow them—you are in the physical world, they are no longer.

▪ Ask for help.
There is a hierarchy in the spirit world, and the ones who have been there the longest, known as the "Exalted Ones," will often come to your aid when asked.

▪ Quickly close the portal.
Make your apologies to the other spirits, quickly recite your portal-closing request, and break hands with your circle.

If none of the above techniques works, see "How to Fend Off a Ghost," p. 100.

HOW TO KNOW WHEN YOU SEE DEAD PEOPLE

Use the following clues to note whether a ghost is present in your immediate environment:

▪ Uncomfortable feelings

A generalized, inexplicable feeling of unease should be your first indicator that a ghost is present.

▪ Changes in temperature

Ghostly presence brings with it a distinct coolness. The room as a whole may be warm (60–70 degrees F), but one area may be very cold (40–50 degrees F) when a ghost is present. Similarly, if most of your body is warm but your arm is very cold, the ghost may be touching your arm.

▪ Physical pressure

Rarely, a ghostly presence can exert an unmistakable physical pressure. If you are performing a séance and feel pressure on your shoulders, you can assume that there are ghosts in the room.

- Audio or visual observation

  Some ghosts make themselves known to an observer, although not necessarily to all observers in the room. Keep your eyes open for visual disturbances and outlines, and listen closely for any subtle, inexplicable sounds.

- Moving objects

  Ghosts will rarely move an object in your presence, but they will tend to move objects when you're not around. If you notice that things are not where you left them—notepads, pencils, keys—you may be in the presence of a ghost. (Do not blame ghosts for every misplaced item, however.)

HOW TO FEND OFF A GHOST

Carol Anne Freeling (Heather O'Rourke): _They're here . . ._
        —Poltergeist

When the TV plays only static and your daughter suddenly gets sucked into the toy closet, it's probably time to battle a ghost. Although poltergeists and spirits usually make themselves known through more subtle means—making blood flow from a faucet, opening cabinets and drawers, possessing the dog—usually the presence of a ghost is downright obvious. The process of ghost busting, as outlined below, is the same whether the ghost is friendly or unfriendly, so trust your own powers and instincts. And if all else fails, feel free to call in the miniature psychics. The information here comes from Tracey, our expert medium.

Step 1: Engage the ghost in conversation.

Oftentimes, and without complicated ritual, a ghost may respond to your direct contact. Ask who it is. Ask what it wants. Ask if there is anything you can do for it. Upon your initial contact, treat the ghost as you would a person. If the ghost refuses conversation, then you are probably dealing with a difficult or harmful spirit, and you may need to get more emphatic.

Step 2: Ask the ghost to leave.

Open a door or a window and ask the ghost to leave. Be sure to keep the threshold clear so that the ghost has an opportunity to exit. The ritual of asking a ghost to leave on your terms, through your thresholds, implies that you have power over it.

Step 3: Hold a séance and ask for help from beyond if the ghost will not leave.

Use the techniques discussed in "How to Contact the Dead" (p. 94), to open a portal. Once the portal is open, ask for help from other spirits related to the ghost. Sometimes a family member can help the ghost to move on to another place.

Step 4: If no family member arrives to help fend off the ghost, ask for help from a higher power.

The spirit world has hierarchies just as in the physical world. With your portal open, request assistance from a higher power. When calling the name "Higher Power," be polite but non-specific. The powers will hear you. They know who they are.

EXORCISING THE GHOST

- **Place a pinch of sea salt in all corners of each room in your house.**
  Let the ghost know that you are going to clean it out of your home. Let the salt sit for 24 hours and then meticulously clean the house—picking up the salt in the corners last. Sea salt has cleansing properties that may help to remove the spirit.

- **Enlist the help of friends in an expulsion ritual.**
  Form a line with several friends, each one holding a stick of incense. Waving your incense, move clockwise around the house. Move through each room and demand that the ghost leave.

- **Invite your religious leader over to bless a small glass of water or other object important to you.**
  Splash the water or move the object around the thresholds of your house. This should purify them and make it difficult for the ghost to move around. (You can do this yourself, if you feel you're religious enough.)

To exorcise a restless spirit move clockwise around the house,
waving sticks of incense.

Step 5: If steps 1 through 4 do not work, attempt to remove the stubborn ghost through ritual.

At this point, fending off the ghost becomes a battle of the wills. You are dealing with a stubborn spirit, so you will need to be stubborn as well. Remove the spirit by using one of the exorcism methods listed on p. 101.

Step 6: When all other actions have been taken, seek the help of a professional ghost buster and get out.

If you have reached this point, you need to be very careful. A strong-willed, angry ghost can be very difficult to handle. Find a local medium or ghost buster and retain their services. (A reliable psychic will be able to refer one to you.) Stay in a hotel or with a friend until your house can be purged and the walls stop bleeding.

Dr. Sam Welzak (Herbert Lom): *Not only can you see the future, you can . . .*
Johnny Smith (Christopher Walken): *I can change it.*
 —*The Dead Zone*

Clairvoyance isn't just a good name for a babe in a secret agent flick—it's also the ability to see things beyond the range of normal human vision, regardless of your prescription. According to mediums, we all have the ability to see the future. Clairvoyance simply eliminates the space between what you can see physically and what the mind's eye can see naturally. In this section, you will learn to look through the physical world to see the answers to your questions. And if you don't find them there, you might want to take a shovel to that suspicious-looking mound out back. The information here was provided by medium and divination arts expert Tracey.

TUNING UP YOUR THIRD EYE

You will need a partner for this exercise.

Step 1: Sit across from your partner and begin to set the proper mood.
Situate yourselves in a comfortable space, indoors or outdoors. Light a candle and set it in the space between you and your partner.

Step 2: Using one of the following methods, take yourselves to a place of sharpened focus.
 ▪ Meditation: Focus your eyes on a candle or an object between

you and your partner. Breathe in through your nose, hold the breath for three seconds, and then breathe out through your mouth for several long breaths.

- Prayer: Use whatever form of prayer your beliefs dictate to focus your energies in the space.

Step 3: Close your eyes.
Have your partner close his or her eyes as well.

Step 4: Practice "throwing" objects to each other.
With your eyes closed, have your partner think of a color, a number, or any other category of items. Use your third eye to "see" what thing your partner is thinking of.

Step 5: Have your partner reveal the object to you.
Be prepared for some initial failures. Success is not instantaneous. The more practice you get, the better you will be able to see.

ALTERNATIVE METHOD: "TAKING" CANDLE FLAMES

Step 1: Light a candle and stare at the flame for one minute.

Step 2: Close your eyes.
You can still see the flame.

Step 3: With your eyes closed, look up and down and side to side.

Step 4: Open your eyes and look around the room.
You can see the room with your eyes. The candle will appear as an overlaying image as you look around the room. This image is viewed by your third eye. You are seeing something that you know is there, without looking directly at it. This is the same technique you will use to see the future.

You are now ready to see the future. Experts compare seeing with your third eye to going to the bathroom in the dark—you know where everything is even though you can't see it.

PREDICTING THE FUTURE

Step 1: Mentally ask a specific question of yourself about the future.

The more specific the question, the more accurate the answer will be. For example, "Will I have $1 million in 10 years?" will get a better response than, "How much money will I have in 10 years?"

Step 2: Focus until you can see the answer.

Take your time. Do not force it. Sometimes a picture—usually an image of an object or place or time—can take a little while to form in your mind's eye. You will be able to feel the answer when it comes.

Step 3: Explore all possibilities of interpretation.

Sometimes you may see—in answer to your question—a color or two. You may see a piece of furniture or the face of an old friend. Allow this image to be what it is. Do not try to force an answer. The first feeling you get—from your instinctual mind's eye—is usually correct. Your old friend may represent anything from the past to a lost love. Trust your interpretations. But leave them loose enough to take on whatever meaning they may hold for you.

Step 4: Set goals based on your visions.

As you move into the future, expect your vision to come true. If your vision is beneficial to you, work toward that goal. If your vision is harmful to you, consider altering your present course of action in an attempt to sway future events.

Step 5: Recheck your vision.

Repeat steps 1 to 3 several days or weeks later to make sure that you are still on the right track.

Step 6: Warn anyone who appears to be in danger according to your vision.

Advise them to take the necessary steps to protect themselves.

HOW TO PERFORM
THE JEDI MIND TRICK

Obi-Wan Kenobi (Alec Guinness): *These aren't the droids you're looking for.*
Stormtrooper: *These aren't the droids we're looking for.*
Obi-Wan Kenobi: *You can go about your business.*
Stormtrooper: *You can go about your business.*
Obi-Wan Kenobi: *Move along.*
Stormtrooper (waving him on): *Move along. Move along.*
      —*Star Wars*

Although Jedi Knights don't really exist, there is a Force that you can tap into to help you influence the behavior of security guards, stormtroopers, bounty hunters, and fat, pig-snouted Gamorrean Guards alike. It's called manipulation. Manipulating your foes can be a powerful tool—it can help you get past border guards, through Imperial blockades, even into bars and nightclubs. But use the trick sparingly—once your foes realize they've been "Jedi'd," it won't work again. The information here comes from Spencer, "The World's Fastest Hypnotist."

Step 1: Gain your subject's trust.

Listen to your subject as he speaks to you. Listen closely to what he says and how he says it. As you listen, begin to imagine what it would be like to be him in every way.

Step 2: Make your subject feel safe.

Be genuine and show an interest in him. Ask him about his life. Where he's from. What he does. Make him feel comfortable. Help him feel that you will not harm him in any way. Smile. Exhibit an open, friendly manner. Look him in the eyes.

Mirror your subject in tone, speech, breathing,
and body language; then subtly take control.

Step 3: Match your subject exactly in his tone, speech patterns, and breathing.

Breathe as he breathes. If he speaks loudly, you should
speak loudly. If he lowers his voice, lower yours. Imitate him in
subtle ways.

Step 4: Begin to mirror your subject's behavior.

Imagine that your subject is looking in a mirror, and that the
mirror is you. If you are sitting together, sit in the same position

he is sitting. As you converse, use the same vocabulary that he uses. But be subtle—you do not want him to notice that you are mirroring him. If he crosses his legs, cross yours. If he shakes his head as he speaks, shake your head the same way. This helps put your subject unconsciously at ease, and allows you to create a silent rapport. People like people who are like them.

Step 5: Attempt to lead your subject's behavior.

You may now be able to influence your subject's behavior by subtly taking control. Begin to lead your subject's movements, breathing, and vocabulary. Notice that he begins to move as you move, breathe as you breathe, and speak as you speak.

Now that you and your subject are in synch, you should be able to take control. First, attempt to take control directly by insisting confidently that your subject give you what you want—say, "Take me to your leader," or "You don't need to see my papers." If this doesn't work, try the more passive approach, suggesting that your subject "may feel like" (in his own time, in his own way) taking you to his leader.

Keep in mind that you must stay flexible. You are sneaking in the back door of your subject's subconscious, so step carefully.

WHEN TO USE THE FORCE

- **People are more suggestible when they are in heightened emotional states.**
  Excite your subject by tapping into his feelings of fear, greed, anger, or love.

- **When performing the Jedi Mind Trick on a small group of people, be the most charismatic person in that group.**
  The majority of people in a group will tend to follow the most boisterous voice in the group.

Guard (as Lone Starr pinches his neck): *What the hell are you doing?*
Lone Starr (Bill Pullman): *The Vulcan Neck Pinch?*
Guard: *No, no, no, stupid, you've got it much too high. It's down here where the shoulder meets the neck.*
Lone Starr (changes hand position): *Like this?*
Guard: *Yeah!* (he falls to the ground)
Lone Starr: *Thanks.*
—*Spaceballs*

When performed correctly, the Vulcan Nerve Pinch can bring to a close any hand-to-hand combat situation or render an unsuspecting guard unconscious within a matter of seconds. In the real world, any action hero with skill and a rudimentary knowledge of pressure points can knock out an opponent. The pinch can be executed by either finger pressure or a direct chop, and both methods are described below. According to Kenka Karate founder Ray Geraneo, the pinch has helped many an action hero live long and prosper.

Step 1: Locate your opponent's radial nerve.

The radial nerve, which helps control the movement and functioning of the arm, is two inches below the elbow joint on top of the forearm.

Step 2: Press your thumb or index knuckle into the radial nerve.

Activating the radial nerve will temporarily paralyze your subject's arm and give you time to activate the brachial plexus tie-in (see step 4), which will paralyze your subject.

If you can get close enough, imbed your thumb into the radial nerve of your subject. Hold and press firmly.

If you need to keep some distance from your subject—if he's holding a weapon, or you need the element of surprise—tuck all of your fingers into a fist. Raise the middle knuckle of your index finger so that it protrudes past the back of your hand. Drive your knuckle into the radial nerve of your subject.

Step 3: Locate the brachial plexus tie-in.

The brachial plexus tie-in, which helps control normal arm function, is about two inches below the shoulder. Find the corner of the pectoral (chest) muscle and move to about one inch above the armpit.

Step 4: Use either your thumb or index finger, as described in step 2, to activate the brachial plexus tie-in.

With pressure still applied to the radial nerve, activate the brachial plexus tie-in with your other hand. This will essentially deaden your opponent's arm and allow you to move in closer.

THE QUICK PINCH

Step 1: Locate the jugular notch.
Feel for the indentation at the base of the throat, in the front, below the Adam's apple. (Locate it on your own body by pushing lightly with two fingers. You should feel your trachea—and a slight gagging sensation.)

Step 2: Strike the jugular notch.
Using your middle and index fingers—either extended straight out or bent at the middle knuckle—strike the jugular notch using a jabbing motion. The strike will cause an immediate gag reflex and motor dysfunction, and allow you time to make your escape if the transporter is malfunctioning.

STRIKE HERE

Use the back of your hand, your forearm, or your knee
to strike the brachial plexus origin and render your subject unconscious.

Step 5: Apply pressure or a chop to the brachial plexus origin.

The brachial plexus origin is found at the base of the neck—at
either side, directly above the collarbone. The carotid artery and
several nerves run up through this area. Activating it through
pressure or a strike can render your subject unconscious.

When quick action is needed, you can simply use the back
of your hand, forearm, or knee—if your subject is low enough—
to strike the origin. A solid and direct hit to the nerve-rich area
should disrupt your opponent's blood flow and render him
unconscious.

CHAPTER 4
Fighting Skills

IT GOES WITHOUT SAYING that every action hero absolutely must know how to fight. But action heroes today encounter so many different kinds of battles that it's often difficult to prepare for what's coming next. One day you may find yourself in a boxing ring, the next in a bar fight against an armed thug, and the next up against an army of ninjas. So it's essential to have a well-rounded fight vocabulary—a good defense and a good offense, the ability to hold your own in a one-on-one street fight and a three-against-one ambush, and a familiarity with gunplay and anything else that might come your way.

That's where this chapter comes in. Here is your primer on the basics of fighting in all situations. You'll learn how to train for a title fight, take a hit with a chair, disarm a thug, and more. You never know what will be resting on the outcome—your life or death, the fate of a loved one, or maybe the free world itself. So be ready. Be strong. Be a hero. Yippee-ki-yay.

Mickey (Burgess Meredith): *For a 45-minute fight, you gotta train hard for 45,000 minutes! 45,000! That's ten weeks, that's ten hours a day—ya' listenin'? And you ain't even trained one! What the hell are you waitin' for, what are you waitin' for?!*
— *Rocky II*

To get in shape for a boxing match and achieve that eye of the tiger, you should expect to work out for at least six months. You should spar about a hundred rounds before you have a competitive fight, and have about 50 competitive fights before you attempt to fight a championship bout. And you can double that if you are defending your country's honor against a gigantic opponent from the former Soviet Union. According to boxing coach Cappy Kotz, you'll need to focus on two primary goals: learning how to box and getting into shape. (Remember to watch out for that uppercut.)

THE FUNDAMENTALS

Begin with your technique. Once your technique is honed, you'll be able to work on acquiring strength. Learn to deliver your punches off your footwork: use your footwork to get close enough to punch your opponent and quickly move out of your opponent's punching range.

Note: The following instructions are written for a right-handed boxer. If you are a southpaw, simply substitute "left" for "right." You may want to wear gloves during your training—just to get used to the feel—but gloves and headgear are not required until you begin sparring.

Step 1: Learn the staggered stance.

Stand with your left foot forward, about a foot-and-a-half away from your right foot. Hold your hands in front of your face at about eyebrow level. Use your left hand to jab and your right as your power hand.

Step 2: Learn to deliver straight punches.

Both the jab and the straight right are delivered to your opponent in a plane, at eyebrow level. The punches are delivered "straight on" to your opponent. Both punches return to position in the same plane. The jab is your staple punch—it sets up your other punches and combinations. You should be able to keep your jab going constantly. Take full advantage of your power when throwing your straight right.

Step 3: Learn the hooks.

Hooks are delivered with your body moving at a slightly twisted angle to the side of your opponent's head and body. To deliver a right hook, pivot left on the ball of the right foot so that your body rotates left. With your right arm bent, carry your punch into the side of your opponent's body or head.

Step 4: Learn uppercuts.

Uppercuts are delivered from a crouched position as you punch up into your opponent's head or body. To deliver an uppercut, use your legs to power a punch up into your opponent's chin or solar plexus. With your legs slightly spread—about waist wide—and your left foot slightly in front of your right, transfer your weight forward and upward from right to left.

Boxing Fundamentals

Staggered Stance

Straight Punch

Hook

Uppercut

Blocking Punches

Step 5: Learn the defensive fundamentals.

- **Blocking punches:** Fold your arms into your body and tighten your back and torso muscles. Hold your hands close to the sides of your head. As your opponent punches other parts of your body, move the position of your arms to block the punches accordingly.

- **Slipping punches:** Shift your weight forward, back, or side to side so that a punch delivered from an opponent misses you. Watch either your opponent's eyes or—peripherally—hands to gauge where his punch is heading. Try both techniques until you can determine which one works best for you.

- **Parrying:** Lightly hit your opponent's punching arm so that the punch is directed away from you. If the punch is coming from your right to your left, aim your punch to the outside of your opponent's left arm. You should be parrying from outside to inside. At the same time turn your left shoulder slightly back and away from the deflected punch.

GETTING IN SHAPE

Focus your energy on preparing for the match by going into a training camp about seven weeks before the bout. Work out six days a week, then rest and prepare mentally for the match. Perform boxing workouts on Monday, Wednesday, and Friday, and roadwork on Tuesday, Thursday, and Saturday. Plan to work out for one to two hours a day, doing each of the following steps:

Step 1: Begin with a cardio workout.

Use the following exercises to begin your cardio workout. In any combination, work eight to ten three-minute sets unless otherwise specified.

- Jump rope and footwork. For three minutes at maximum output, jump continuously on two feet and then alternate from left foot only to right foot only.
- Ply metrics. For three minutes at maximum output, with both feet planted, jump laterally over a cone or series of cones. Jump and land with your weight evenly distributed on both feet.
- Medicine ball. Holding the medicine ball to your chest with

TRAINING TIPS

- **Learn to equate food with fuel.**
  Eat small meals every three to four waking hours in the following combinations: 55 to 65 percent complex carbohydrates, 20 to 30 percent fats, 15 to 20 percent protein. Avoid fried foods, refined sugar products, and excessive alcohol intake.

- **Control your emotions.**
  Learn not to react to emotional ups and downs both inside and outside the ring. The more you can stay at an even keel, the more precise your technique will be. Work on your psychological training by not letting your emotions get in the way of your fighting.

- **Sex is OK (more than OK) up to one week before your title bout.**
  Do not engage in any wild drug- or alcohol-related sexual activity at any time during your training. Spend your final week of training focusing solely on boxing—not sex.

THE CHAMPIONSHIP DIET

You should eat a small meal every three to four hours.

8AM: Water, juice, cereal or bagel, coffee.
12PM: Water, one or two sandwiches with meat, soup, and carrot sticks, or pasta and red sauce with meat and carrot sticks.
4PM: Water, rice, vegetables, and beans.
8PM: Water, stew, bread, and a glass of wine, beer, or water, or potatoes, baked chicken, salad, and a glass of beer or wine.

your elbows out to your sides, use your back to deliver a
chest pass back and forth to a partner. Accept his pass with
your arms, chest, and back. Pass the ball for three minutes
at maximum output.

- Stretch for five to seven minutes.
    - Hamstring stretch. From a standing position, stretch your
      left leg straight out in front of you and rest it on a table or
      chair (about waist high). Push down on your thigh gently,
      and bend forward at the waist (toward your knee) until your
      leg is straight. Hold for 20 seconds, release, and stretch
      your other leg.
    - Quadriceps stretch. From a standing position, bend your left
      leg at the knee and use your left hand to pull your left foot
      toward your rear end. Hold for 20 seconds, release, and
      stretch your other leg.
    - Shoulder stretch. From a standing position, extend your left
      arm across your chest and press it close to your chest with
      your right forearm. Hold for 20 seconds, release, and stretch
      your other shoulder.

Step 2: **Move to pad work.**

Focus on working your punch combinations and defensive tactics
(see pp. 117–19). You should do six rounds of drills or actual sparring. Spar in three-minute rounds with a one-minute rest between
each round, concentrating on your punches and footwork.

Step 3: **Perform calisthenics and weight training.**

Do crunches (3 sets of 100), push-ups (3 sets of 25), pull-ups (3
sets of 15), back-ups (3 sets of 20), bench presses (3 sets of 10
light weight, focusing on form), biceps curls (3 sets of 20 light
weight), and triceps extensions (3 sets of 15 light weight).

Step 4: Hit the road.

For 1 to 1½ hours, perform roadwork on a track or dirt path. Line up your stride and set a constant, easy jogging pace. A ten-minute mile is a consistent gait.

Interrupt the pace by climbing inclines or stairs, but always return to your constant pace.

Dalton (Patrick Swayze): *Pain don't hurt.*
        —Road House

A good fighter not only knows how to hit, but how to take a hit—a skill that's especially handy when you're in a particularly rough bar or saloon (and you will be). Tempers usually fly in a barfight, but tempers alone don't hurt. However, solid oak chairs or barstools cracked over your head do. According to stuntman Christopher Caso, the key to taking a hit with a chair is knowing when to duck and when to take cover—as well as when to walk away and when to run.

Note: Getting hit with a chair from behind, or from any side by a metal chair, will inflict a significant amount of pain and injury. Use the techniques in "How to Be Ready for Anything" (p. 130) to help defuse a situation and the techniques in "How to Win a Fight When You're Outnumbered" (p. 133) to try to dodge either a metal chair or one coming from behind.

IF THE CHAIR IS MADE OF WOOD

Getting hit with a wooden chair is going to hurt no matter what you do, but if you see it coming, and you have protected yourself properly, the hit will cause little permanent damage. It is most important to protect vital areas and absorb the impact where it will cause the least amount of damage.

Step 1: Cover your head.

Put your arms up—fists just above your head, forearms in front of your face—to protect your face and head. Tilt your head away from the oncoming chair.

Step 2: Turn your body to the side.
Do not turn so that your back accepts the blow! Swivel your body so that the chair will hit only your arm, shoulder, and side.

Step 3: Tuck your body as much as possible to protect your vital organs.
Remember that bones and ligaments will heal better than organ tissue. Tuck your body so that your muscles compact around your kidneys and other vital organs.

Step 4: Go with the flow of the blow.
As the chair comes toward you, follow the defensive measures above, then move in the direction of the hit to lessen the impact. If the chair is coming from above, accept the hit and drop to the ground as soon as the chair touches you. If it is coming from the side, move your body so that it follows the chair's trajectory.

Step 5: If you can drop to the ground before the chair comes at you, do so.
Fall onto your back, bringing your feet up to protect your body and accept the impact of the hit. Use your legs as shock absorbers and extend them toward the hit. As soon as the chair makes contact with your legs, allow them to bend and "give."

IF THE CHAIR IS MADE OF METAL
You should do everything you can to avoid getting hit with a metal (particularly steel) chair. However, if a hit is unavoidable, follow these steps:

Cover your head, turn to the side, and go with the flow of the blow.

Step 1: Get to the ground.

Your best bet for minimizing injury from a steel chair hit is to get to the ground and bring your feet up to protect your body.

Step 2: Use your legs to absorb the blow.

Extend your legs toward the hit. As soon as the chair makes contact with your legs, let them bend and "give" to accept the blow.

Step 3: Use your legs to deflect the blow.

As your legs bend and "give," move them and the chair away from your body. Think of it as using your legs to "guide" the chair away from your vital organs.

Kid (Leonardo DiCaprio): *You see, it's a gunfight. We both have guns. We aim. We fire. You die.*
> —The Quick and the Dead

Even contemporary action heroes find themselves in an Old West–type shoot-out every now and then. Sure, a lot of today's outlaws wear black Armani suits instead of black hats, and many wear their guns up their sleeves or under their jackets instead of on their hips. But whether you're in a gunfight with a maniacal android cowboy in an amusement park gone haywire or in a slo-mo shoot-out on motorcycles at the climax of your impossible mission, you'll certainly need to know how to draw and shoot. The information here comes from Fast Draw World Champion Howard Darby.

Use one of the techniques described below to draw your gun and fire. The more you practice, the more you will be able to reduce unnecessary movements and unpredictable gun travel.

THE SLAP-COCK DRAW

Step 1: Get your hands in the correct position.

You should use your dominant hand to hold and fire the gun. Place your dominant hand close to the gun on your hip holster. Get ready to place the last three fingers of your hand around the handle (but do not touch it yet), so that they can quickly grab and draw. Your index finger should be directly above the trigger guard, ready to be inserted when you hear the word "draw."

Place your other hand directly above the hammer of the gun in its holster so that your index finger is in place to fan the hammer.

Gunfighter's rule: Do not touch any part of the gun until you hear "draw," or until the bad guy draws.

Step 2: On "draw," close the fingers of your dominant hand around the handle of the gun.

Simultaneously, with your other hand, pull back the hammer and cock the gun. This move should take less than a tenth of a second.

Step 3: Remove the gun from the holster.

Pull the handle of the gun from the holster so that the nose is still pointing downward. As you do so, insert your trigger finger—usually your index finger—into the trigger.

Step 4: Get the gun into shooting position.

You only need to clear the nose of the gun past the leather and point it toward your opponent to squeeze off the shot—do not worry about elevating it any higher. Aim as soon as the nose of the gun is clear of the holster, and be ready to shoot from the hip.

Depending on your opponent—and your skill—you can aim for any part of your opponent's body. The key in quick draw, however, is to be the first one to draw, shoot, and hit your target. It is very difficult to draw and hit a specific target—hand, knee, shoulder—at high speed. So just focus on the big picture.

Step 5: Pull the trigger and fire the gun.

You will be allowed only one shot—unless your opponent has enemies aiming a rifle at you from above the general store.

The Thumbing Draw

1. Place hand near gun with thumb over hammer.

2. On "draw," fan hammer with thumb.

3. Remove gun from holster.

4. Aim and shoot.

THE THUMBING DRAW

This is a one-handed draw in which the thumb of the firing hand is used to fan the hammer while the index finger of the same hand pulls the trigger.

Step 1: Place your hand near the gun.

Using your dominant hand, place your thumb over and parallel to the hammer of the gun. Place the last three fingers of your hand so that they can grab the handle of the gun and draw. Your index finger should again be directly outside the trigger guard.

Step 2: On "draw," fan the hammer with your thumb and close the fingers of your dominant hand around the handle of the gun.

You should bring your thumb straight down on the hammer and cock it with the ball of your thumb. This move should take less than a tenth of a second.

Step 3: Put the gun in shooting position.

Remove the gun from the holster, clear the nose of the gun past the leather, aim, and shoot from the hip.

TIPS TO PRACTICE BEFORE HIGH NOON

- **As you discover which draw works best for you, practice the moves again and again so that they become second nature.**
As you practice you will begin to "know" where you have to be in order to hit the target. When the time comes, you'll automatically line up for the draw and can devote your concentration to the draw itself. Trust that if you are lined up right, you will hit your target.

- **Be careful: Both drawing techniques require that the gun be cocked before it's clear of the holster.**
Beware of your own friendly fire, and wear steel-toed boots just in case.

John McClane (Bruce Willis): *Yippee-ki-yay motherf—r.*
— *Die Hard*

As an action hero, you must be ready for anything—anywhere, at anytime. You never know when the bad guys are going to decide to crash the office holiday party, when the mob is going to hit your restaurant, or when that nice little old lady is going to remove her latex mask and sucker punch you. But if you know what to look for, you can anticipate a "situation" before it happens, early enough to develop your defensive strategies. The guidance here comes from confrontation consultant Andrew Netschay.

Step 1: Be suspicious of everyone and everything—but don't let on that you are suspicious.

Instinct is a powerful tool—learn to use yours well. Look around the room. If everyone is having a good time except for one guy in the corner who's scowling at everyone he can see, be suspicious. Look for anything out of the ordinary or out of place—a long trench coat in July, for example.

Step 2: Always make a mental note of exits and entrances to any building you enter.

You may need to use them later.

Step 3: Be aware of what's happening around you.

Trust your powers of observation and peripheral vision. When you come to the moment of confrontation, your eyes will react more acutely. Always take note of what's around you and behind you, where people's hands are, and so forth. The more you can determine "what's wrong with this picture," the better prepared you will be.

Step 4: Control and utilize your fear.

Fear can be a powerful tool as well as a crippling emotion. Recognize the symptoms of fear—sweaty palms, dry mouth, and accelerated pulse—to know when adrenaline is pumping through your system.

Adrenaline is a key indicator—frequently an unconscious one— that something is amiss. You can use it to drug your body into action. Tap into your flow of adrenaline and allow it to influence your behavior. Your mind may say, "This is nuts," but your body will say, "It's so crazy it just might work."

Note: Do not, however, let the adrenaline take over; otherwise, you risk the onset of panic. Keep your breathing steady and balanced and focus on the task at hand—one thing at a time. Try to control your thoughts of the future (i.e., the potential consequences of your situation).

THE THREE HABITS OF HIGHLY EFFECTIVE ACTION HEROES

- **If you can't see one or both of your opponent's hands, assume they are going for a weapon and act accordingly: either disarm your opponent (see "How to Disarm a Thug with a Gun," p. 137) or get out of there.**

- **Notice your opponent's weight distribution and stance. If your opponent is standing with his right fist back and his left side forward, watch for the right side sucker punch. A weight shift from one foot to the other may indicate a kick is on its way.**

- **Stay loose and keep your hands at shoulder level, with your palms facing your opponent. It is easier to block a punch or a grab with your open hand than with your fist.**

Step 5: Don't get caught off guard.

If you have to remove your shoes or shirt to bind a wound or set your weapon down to rig a booby trap, do so very cautiously—it's usually at this moment that criminals make their move, leaving you shirtless, shoeless, and weapon-free.

Step 6: If you must engage in a physical confrontation, attempt to stun your opponent with a finger gouge or throat chop and end the fight quickly.

Unless you are a fifth-degree black belt, do your best to end the physical confrontation as quickly as possible. Use quick and direct strikes to the throat and/or eyes. Push your fingers (or a hand) straight into your opponent's eye or aim for the throat, just above the Adam's apple. The straight shot will give him less time to react.

Step 7: Stay on the move.

Once you have "stopped" your opponent, get out of there. There's no need to stick around—unless you need to save somebody. You'll live to fight another day.

Step 8: Pick up useful items after you've disabled your opponents.

Many an action hero has been caught unarmed simply because he or she neglected to pick up the weapon, uniform, or equipment of the enemy he or she has just dispatched or knocked out. Useful items include:

- Guns, knives, or other weapons
- Equipment bags with tools, flashlights, and other items
- Walkie-talkies
- Uniforms
- Key cards

Det. James Carter (Chris Tucker) (surrounded by thugs): *Stand back. Give me some room. You don't know who you messin' with, I'm not that*—(one of the thugs kicks Carter in the face). *Which one of ya'll kicked me?*
    —*Rush Hour*

The most important thing to learn about being outnumbered in a fight is this: unless you are a well-trained martial arts master who does his own stunts and just recently learned English, you do not win a fight of this nature. You survive it. Even the best martial artists say that, without a doubt, the best way to survive an unfair fight of any kind is to find a way out. And fast. So always look for an escape hatch—an exit or apology, if possible—or just a way to live to fight another day. The information here comes from Kenka Karate founder Ray Geraneo.

SURVIVING THE FIGHT

Step 1: Never allow yourself to be surrounded.
   Keep moving at all times. Move to the outside angle of your opponents' blind spots. A moving target is hard to hit.

Step 2: Keep your opponents lined up.
   Try to position yourself so that your opponents are in line with each other. This way it will be easier to fight them one at a time or use one as a shield against the other.

To Win a Fight:

1. Never let yourself be surrounded.

2. Keep your opponents in a line.

3. Bob and weave.

4. Strike fast and hard.

5. Create a distraction and make your escape.

PREPARING FOR BATTLE

- **Know your combat ranges.**
  There are different ranges for engagement, and in true combat, there is no time to think about shifting from one range to another. You must know your ranges and move from one to the next quickly and instinctively.

  - **Trapping Range: Direct contact. The tools for this range are wristlock or headlock.**

  - **Close Range: Within 12 inches of your body. The tools for this range are elbows, knees, and head-butts.**

  - **Middle Striking Range: Within 24 inches. The tools for this range are punches and open-hand techniques.**

  - **Kicking or Long Range: Within 48 inches. The tools for this range are the front kick and the side kick (and pool cues).**

  - **Grappling Range: Farther than arm's or leg's reach. The tools for this range are shooting and tackling.**

- **Know your environment.**
  Be aware of anything around you—bar stools, bottles, baseball bats, ladders—that could be used as weapons by you or against you.

- **Develop and use "Situational Awareness."**
  "Situational Awareness" is determined by your five senses. Sight, sound, touch, smell, and taste should all be in play. For example, train your vision to stay sharp. Never fixate on one opponent. Train your hearing to key into potential attacks behind you. Keep your nose sharp if you smell someone coming at you with a flame-thrower or other odorific weapon. Do not, however, taste your opponents. Instead, use your sense of taste to gauge the flow of adrenalin—which produces a slightly metallic flavor.

Step 3: Never settle into in one spot, and never allow your opponents to get settled.

Shift your weight and position from side to side. Bob and weave and move around the room. This will keep your opponents from creating a plan of attack, and will make you harder to pin down.

The last place you want to be in a multiple attack situation is on the ground.

Step 4: If you must fight, strike fast and hard and move away quickly.

Use your knowledge of positional ranges (see p. 135) to strike the first opponent and then move again to stay out of their reach and keep your opponents lined up. The odds are already against you, so let go of any ideas you have about fighting fair. Use any improvised weapons around you to improve your odds—chairs, bottles, rocks, and so forth.

Step 5: Identify your method of escape early on in the fight, and use it when the time is right.

You may need to be creative—throwing yourself down a trash chute, sliding down the side of a building, or swinging to safety on a large hanging banner in order to get away. You can count on your opponents to block the standard exits (doors, cars, roof ladders), so look for the nonstandard exits, and take them when the opportunity arrives.

Step 6: Create a sizable distraction and use *time framing* to make your escape.

When you have three people in front of you and you say, "Move!" they will not all move in the same direction at the same time. Use this principle (called *time framing*) to your advantage to create a window of escape. Look for the lag in your opponents' reactions, find your window of escape, and run through it. Start the log-cutting machine, topple a row of shelves, or simply toss garbage cans to throw your opponents off guard and make them scatter. Then get out.

HOW TO DISARM A THUG WITH A GUN

Bug (Vincent D'Onofrio): *Put your projectile weapon on the ground.*
Edgar (Vincent D'Onofrio): *You can have my gun when you pry it from my cold dead hands.*
Bug: *Your proposition is acceptable.*
      —Men in Black

Usually, when approached by a thug with a gun, it is best to avoid confrontation and give the thug what he or she requests. However, in a life-or-death situation, your only option may be to attempt to disarm your opponent. It's not as easy as it looks on paper, so you may want to practice this a few times with a friend, loved one, or the comic sidekick of your choice. Perform the following steps very quickly, in less than a second, and all in one motion. This information was provided by personal security trainer Shawn Engbrecht.

Note: The directions below apply to a right-handed thug. Reverse them if the gun handler is a southpaw.

Step 1: **Quickly move to the thug's right and turn sideways.**
Leading with your left foot, step diagonally toward your thug and turn your body perpendicular to the thug's body. Leave your right leg where it is and pivot on it. You should now be positioned to the outside of your thug—and out of the line of fire—with his right shooting arm directly in front of you.

Step 2: **Lock the thug's right wrist in your left hand.**
With your palm facing down, grab around your thug's wrist where the meat of his thumb and wrist come together. Use your entire

To Disarm a Thug:

1. Move parallel to the gun.

2. Lock thug's wrist with left hand.

3. Grab the gun barrel with right hand.

4. Break thug's trigger finger.

5. Push gun straight down to disarm thug.

hand. Your thumb and forefinger should be around the point where your thug's wrist and hand pivot up and down.

Step 3: Grab the barrel of the gun with your right hand.
With your palm facing up, grab the barrel of the gun from underneath. Use your entire hand and grip the barrel so that your fingers are around it and not in front of it.

Step 4: Break the thug's trigger finger by simultaneously pushing down on your thug's wrist with your left hand and pulling up on the gun barrel with your right.
The gun should be now pointing directly up at the sky and your thug's trigger finger should be broken.

Step 5: Remove the gun from the thug's hand.
Now push straight down toward the ground with your right hand. The gun will slip out of your thug's hand.

Step 6: With gun in hand, step out of the thug's arm's reach.
Hold the weapon on your opponent and subdue him at gunpoint.

THE ELEMENT OF SURPRISE

- As a general rule, when a person pulls and fires a gun in a large crowd of people, nearly everyone will drop to the floor. The thug expects this. If you are at close range to the thug, a sudden and aggressive lunge toward him may throw him off-guard and give you more time to disarm him.

- Use the same technique to disarm a thug with a knife, but beware: You will most likely get cut when performing this move.

CHAPTER 5
Escape Skills

WINNING THE FIGHT, getting the girl (or guy), catching the bad guy, and saving the world is all well and good—but don't break out the champagne and caviar just yet. Because most often, even if the situation is resolved and the plot thwarted, you will still find yourself behind enemy lines.

Our final lesson, therefore, is about getting out of Dodge, sneaking across the border, outrunning the posse, or otherwise making your way to safety. Sometimes you will make your escape alone, sometimes you'll do it with your partner or loved one—but in any case, you need to know how to find your way out of hostile territory (so that you can return for the sequel someday).

Within this section, you'll learn how to evade enemy planes in hot pursuit, navigate a ventilation shaft, slip out of town unnoticed, catch the guy with the parachute in midair, and escape from handcuffs, among other things. Then you can smile, make one more closing smart-ass quip, and relax as the credits roll.

"Maverick" Mitchell (Tom Cruise): *I feel the need . . .*
Maverick and "Goose" Bradshaw (Anthony Edwards): *. . . the need for speed.*
—*Top Gun*

When pursued by MiGs in enemy airspace, your first order of business is managing the energy of your plane, then evading your pursuers. To fly like a top gun, you first need to "sucker" your pursuers into losing control of their craft, and then destroy them or simply fly back to safety. The skill set is the same if you have stolen one of two secret Russian prototype warplanes and are being chased by the other—get in, get what you want, and most importantly, get out. The information here comes from stunt pilot Walt Addison Linscott.

CREATING A PREFLIGHT DISTRACTION

Be sure that your plane is ready for takeoff. If you are stealing a plane, stake out the ground crew and scout a plane that has been serviced and fueled.

Step 1: Draw fuel from the sumps in the wings of your small plane.
The sumps of most small jets, such as an F-series fighter, are at the low point of the wing, underneath the fuselage. Press up on the valve stem to release a steady stream of fuel into a gallon-size plastic or metal canister.

Step 2: Stuff a rag into the end of the canister.

Step 3: Place the canister away from your plane.
The farther away, the better. Take the canister to the other side of the airplane hanger so that the distraction occurs opposite the direction of your escape route.

Step 4: Set the rag on fire and run back to your plane.
Jet fuel and aviation gas burn very quickly and create a lot of smoke. You should have enough time to start your plane and begin your escape while the ground crew struggles to put out the fire.

EVADING A MiG

Step 1: Move into a nap of the earth navigation.

At the highest speed your plane can fly, move into a low-to-the-earth course (known as *nap of the earth* navigation). Stay as close to the treetops or as far down in a canyon as you can fly safely. Try to stay below the line of sight of your enemy's radar. As long as you have terrain between you and your enemy's radar, you will be out of his range.

Step 2: If your enemy finds you, climb to a fair altitude.

Pull back on the control stick until your plane climbs to a reasonable altitude. The required altitude for the following move will depend mostly on your plane. As a general rule, climb high enough to recover from (pull out of) a nearly inverted dive if things go wrong (around 10,000 feet).

Step 3: Move into a high-speed dive.

As you climb, push your control stick to the far left or right and move into an inverted roll. Now pull on the control stick and force the nose toward the ground. This will send you into your dive.

Step 4: Bank hard to the left or right and pull back on the control stick.

Step 5: Roll to wings level and begin to climb.

When the wings of the plane are parallel to the earth, it is known as *wings level*. Slowly pull back on the control stick. This will begin your climb and slowly bleed off your plane speed.

To Evade a MiG:

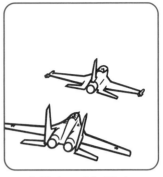

1. Use nap of the earth navigation.

2. Climb to a fair altitude.

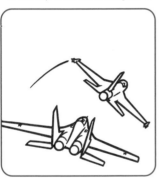

3. Bank hard to the right.

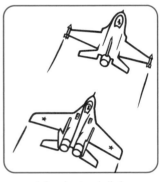

4. Level out and climb.

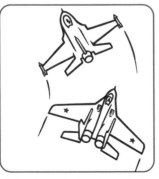

5. Roll left at the top of your climb.

6. Make your escape.

Step 6: Move out at the top of the climb and roll to the left.

At the top of the climb—when your plane has just about reached the edge of its flying capability—roll to the left by pushing the control stick to the left.

This move sets your pursuer up to follow you into what he believes is another inverted dive.

Step 7: Instead of falling into the dive, this time push forward on the stick and continue your climb.

As you push in on your stick, you will climb harder instead of falling faster. Your pursuer will be caught off guard by this shift of direction and speed and should fall into a spin.

Step 8: As your pursuer spins, return to the nap of the earth and make your escape at full throttle.

Roll to a level position and begin to dive. When you have picked up speed again, continue down to the treetops to make your escape. Your enemy will be unlikely to catch up.

INVERTED TAUNTING

If you really want to mess with your pursuer, perform the following maneuver inverted over the top of his plane. For this move you will be upside down but directly over your pursuer—so that if you leaned your head back toward the earth you could see him.

Step 1: Fly directly above your pursuer.

Come up from behind your opponent. You may have to sneak up on him through some cloud cover. Climb to a position directly over his plane.

Step 2: Adjust your speed to match his plane's speed.

Step 3: Push the nose of your plane slightly upward.
Create a little "back pressure" on your control stick—pull it back and slightly toward your feet—to achieve this. This will prepare you for your roll and will keep the nose of your plane up, as it will otherwise tend to fall toward the horizon.

Step 4: Push your control stick to the left or right and roll to an inverted position.
Make sure there is sufficient vertical distance between planes as you roll. The distance should be about twice the width of your plane's wingspan.

Step 5: Press the nose of your plane back up.
Relax the back pressure on your stick and push forward on it to create some forward pressure. This will force the nose up in the inverted position.

Step 6: Slowly pull back on the stick a little to lower your plane over your enemy's cockpit.
Push forward a little to go up if you get too close. Remember that the control inputs are the reverse of flying right-side up, so be careful. Do not let your plane get any closer than four feet from your pursuer's—your tails might hit each other.

Step 7: Taunt him as you wish.
Visual contact may be your only option. Just let him know who's "Number 1."

HOW TO FIX
YOUR SPACE SHUTTLE
ON REENTRY

Jim Lovell (Tom Hanks): *Houston, we have a problem.*
      —Apollo 13

Luckily for the modern-day space-exploring action hero, most systems on the space shuttle are automated. However, there are those rare times when things go awry—like when that evil multimillionaire bent on world domination damages your orbital maneuvering systems. At those times, it's helpful to know how to escape danger and execute a de-orbit burn with your manual backup systems. According to Flight Dynamics Officer Lisa B. Shore, this will slow your velocity enough so that you begin to fall out of orbit and back to earth (where you can safely land)—and give you just enough time to put the moves on that sexy doctor onboard.

Step 1: Turn the shuttle around.

Using the control stick, start a three-degree-per-second pitch-up maneuver until you are completely turned over. If you were heads down—tail to the earth—when you started your move, you should pitch until you are belly down.

Step 2: Fire your OMS engines.

Your orbital maneuvering system (OMS) engines are in the rear of the shuttle. Press the keypad buttons to control the onboard general-purpose computers (GPCs) and engage these engines. The OMS engines will slow you down and drop the shuttle back toward earth. As the shuttle slows, make sure its nose faces away from the direction of travel.

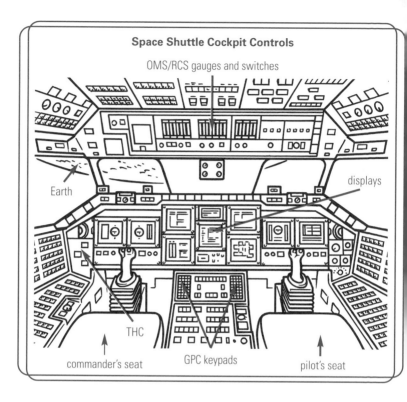

Space Shuttle Cockpit Controls

OMS/RCS gauges and switches

Earth

displays

THC

commander's seat

GPC keypads

pilot's seat

If your OMS engines do not fire (you will notice that your velocity has not decreased), you need to remain backward to fire the aft reaction control system (RCS) jets.

Step 3: Prepare to fire the RCS jets by opening the valve that controls the flow of the rear engine's propellant.

This will switch the propellant from the OMS engines to the aft RCS jets. The panels, keyboards, and displays that operate the computer are directly between the pilot's and the commander's seats.

Step 4: Fire the aft RCS jets.

Push in on the translational hand controller (THC) to fire the aft jets. Fire the jets until almost all of the propellant is used. This should slow you down greatly.

Note: YOU MUST SAVE SOME PROPELLANT FOR THE AFT RCS JETS FOR A LATER MOVE, SO DO NOT USE IT ALL! The RCS gauges, located on the overhead panel between the pilot's and the commander's seats, will give you the proper propellant reading. A toggle switch will allow you to switch between the OMS gauge and the RCS gauge.

Step 5: Turn the shuttle around again, using the control stick.

The shuttle should now be facing forward, still belly-down.

Step 6: Fire the forward RCS jets.

Pull out on the THC to fire the forward jets. Use the jets to slow you down even more. The forward jets will not fire as long as the aft jets, but don't worry—the tanks on the front are much smaller.

Step 7: Use the atmosphere to slow you down even more.

Bank the shuttle to a 40-degree, belly-to-the-earth, nose-up position. At about 400,000 feet altitude, begin your prebank maneuver. The shuttle will continue to move forward through the atmosphere, but the nose-up position will increase the drag and expose the thermal protection system (TPS) to the heat of the atmosphere.

Step 8: Hold this position until you reach about 250,000-feet altitude.

At this point, guidance from ground control will start actively aiming you toward the landing site.

Step 9: Ride the shuttle home.

Butch Cassidy (Paul Newman): *They can't track us over rocks.*
The Sundance Kid (Robert Redford) (pointing to posse): *Tell them that.*
Butch (looks at posse, dumfounded): *Who ARE those guys?*
    —*Butch Cassidy and the Sundance Kid*

To make a getaway, you need to simultaneously stay sharp but look ordinary. In fact, looking anonymous is the key to slipping across the border, out of the state, or out of the country. Try to blend in as much as possible. Try not to look too fancy or too cheap. Try not to do anything that will make you stand out in a crowd. And no matter what, don't ever—we repeat, ever—fall in love. (The last rule doesn't really apply to this skill, but it's a good one just the same.) The information here comes from personal security trainer Shawn Engbrecht.

PASSING UNNOTICED AT THE AIRPORT

If you sense you're being tailed by the bad guys in an airport, use the following evasive techniques.

Step 1: Make as little eye contact as possible.
   When you make eye contact with people, you imprint your image on their memory. Do not make eye contact with anyone in a crowd.
      You *should*, however, make eye contact—only momentarily—with security guards or personnel manning checkpoints. Avoiding eye contact with authority figures raises suspicion.

PREPARING FOR ESCAPE

▪ Wear drab clothes.
Wear only light blues, grays, or tans to blend in to the crowd.

▪ Tone down your hairstyle.
Don't go in for a funky hairstyle. Get a plain haircut if you are a man or wear your hair at shoulder length if you are a woman.

▪ Use some simple techniques to quickly change your appearance.
Use shoe polish to change your hair color, wear a wig or a hat, and alter your gait.

Step 2: Speak to no one—or to as few people as possible.

Again, when you speak to people you give them more to remember about you. Do not speak to anyone in a crowd. Speak as little as possible to security guards or checkpoint personnel.

Step 3: Do not do anything out of the ordinary.

Think of yourself as a shoe salesman returning home from a conference. You are at the airport, reading the paper, waiting to get on your plane and fly home to your wife, dog, and 2.5 children. Do not draw attention to yourself in any way.

Step 4: Subdue your walking style.

A walk of authority—with your shoulders back and your head up—will attract attention. Hunch your shoulders slightly and look at the floor as you walk. This indicates that you are not a threat to anyone.

Warning: Do not overdo your subdued walk. Try to look natural, shy, and meek rather than suspicious, coy, and sly. And no limping.

Step 5: Get into the middle of the line when boarding a plane.
Never be the first or last person on or off the aircraft. Get on right in the middle when boarding begins.

Step 6: Hide in the lavatory before departure.
After you place your things near your seat, casually go to the bathroom. If you've managed to shake your pursuer, he or she won't know where you're seated, and will have to get off the plane before it leaves. Be sure to take your seat before the flight attendant does a head count.

FAKING OUT PURSUERS AT THE TRAIN STATION

If you are aware that you are being followed by enemies, try to shake them off your trail.

Step 1: In the station, take an escalator or elevator up and then right back down.
If you notice someone doing the same, he is following you.

Step 2: Get on the wrong train.
Step onto a train other than the one you mean to take. Just as the train begins to move, hop off onto the platform. Keep your eyes open at this point. If someone else hops off the train and onto the platform, he is most likely after you.

Step 3: Get on your train a few cars ahead of your pursuer.
Be sure that he sees which car you got on. He will be moving forward, toward your position.

Step 4: In between cars, moving forward and away from your pursuer, climb up onto the top of the train.

Making sure that no one sees you, use the ladder handholds to climb up the side. Once on top of the train, begin to walk back toward your pursuer's general direction.

Warning: This maneuver is not recommended when the train is in motion.

Step 5: Walk back several cars and then climb back into the train.

Climb down the side opposite the platform, using the ladder handholds, and enter the train car. Your pursuer should be in front of you at this point and probably will hop off the train when he gets to the front without finding you.

Step 6: Return to the back of the train and hide in a lavatory.

After the train begins to move, you may assume that your pursuer has stepped off the train. If you get caught on the train without a ticket, use one of the following tactics to get out of trouble:

- Pretend to be asleep.
- Pretend you do not speak English.

If you get kicked off the train, no worries. You've still evaded your pursuer.

Thelma Dickinson (Geena Davis): *Are you sure we should be driving like this, I mean in broad daylight and everything?*

Louise Sawyer (Susan Sarandon): *No, we shouldn't, but I want to put some distance between us and the scene of our last goddamn crime.*
　　　—Thelma and Louise

All action heroes worth their salt will know how to win a high-speed car chase—either as the one fleeing or pursuing. When fleeing, the key to staying in the lead is to take your pursuers places they may not likely go: through narrow alleys, across busy intersections, or down extremely steep hills in San Francisco. As the pursuer, you must capitalize on your quarry's mistakes. If you drive as outlined below, according to demolition driver Vinny Minchillo, nine times out of ten the person you are chasing will slip up.

IF YOU'RE CHASING

Step 1: Use the fleeing person's stress against him.

The person you are chasing is under a lot of stress, just by the nature of the position you've put him in. He is most likely not making clear decisions. You can use this to force him down the wrong path.

Step 2: Drive calmly and smoothly—but quickly.

Driving well requires calm, smooth movements. Use very slight inputs on the steering wheel and pedals. It is easier to add more turn to a wheel than it is to recover from turning too much.

Step 3: Anticipate what lies ahead.

Look down the road and anticipate situations. You should make a plan for weaving through the thick traffic rather than reacting at the last second. Plot the course ahead in your mind, and then smoothly move through it.

Step 4: Don't focus on the fleeing vehicle—watch the horizon.

Traveling at high speed, it's better to look ahead to the horizon than to focus on your fleeing vehicle. This will allow you to take in the big picture as you drive. You should be able to see your quarry as well as potential oncoming threats—like grandmas inching across the crosswalk or fish trucks backing across the alley.

Step 5: Take corners by braking before you enter the turn from the outside lane, then accelerating through the corner.

Turn your wheel so that you shift to the inside lane of the corner as you move through it, then slowly open up and accelerate out of the corner.

Step 6: When you come close to your subject's car, stay close and wait for him to make a mistake.

The longer the chase goes on, the better chance the fleeing person has to escape. Get close to the rear bumper and swing back and forth so that you appear in both of his mirrors. The more time he spends looking in his mirrors, the less time his eyes are on the road, and the more likely it is he will make an error in judgment, allowing you to take control.

Step 7: Hit the fleeing car in the rear bumper.

Banging the bumper will serve several purposes. It will slow the vehicle down, frazzle the driver, and upset the car's handling. If you perform this move on a turn you may potentially spin the vehicle out. BUT BE CAREFUL! YOU MAY ALSO SPIN YOURSELF OUT.

Step 8: Try to stop the fleeing vehicle.

Try to force the driver to make a mistake that will cause him to spin out. Come up behind the car and put your front corner—either driver's or passenger's side—up against the space between the rear wheel and the rear bumper of the fleeing car. Turn toward the car while simultaneously stepping on the gas.

Once he's spun out, quickly stop your car against the driver's side door to make sure he doesn't escape. (See "How to Win a High-Speed Chase on Foot," p. 158.)

IF YOU'RE FLEEING

The key to winning a high-speed chase if you are being pursued is . . . don't make mistakes. In a high-speed chase, the first mistake loses.

- Be calm and smooth in your driving.

  Decide where and how you want the car to go and then execute. Stay committed to the maneuver.

- Don't let your pursuers get close enough to your car to make you spin you out (see above).

  You may have a natural tendency to speed up if they attempt to come alongside you. Instead, use your brakes to outmaneuver them. No one said a chase always has to move forward.

- Head to familiar territory.

  If you can get to an area that you are familiar with, do it. Go through garages or alleys to confuse your pursuers.

- Use traffic to put space between you and your pursuers.

  Carefully weave in and out of other traffic on a highway. Move to the inside lane. Wait until your pursuer is a few cars back in the

Brake before entering the turn, then accelerate through the corner.

same lane. Check traffic and—if it's clear—speed across the lanes and onto an exit ramp. Your pursuer may not have access to the same traffic patterns and will be unable to follow.

- Keep your options open.

  You don't have to race at breakneck speeds. Use the car to move ahead or fall behind your pursuer. If you find that you are racing through narrow streets and tight places, head to an open highway to give yourself more choices.

Dr. Szell (Laurence Olivier): *Is it safe?*
Babe (Dustin Hoffman): *Yes. Yes, it's safe. It's so safe you wouldn't believe it.*
    —*Marathon Man*

Being pursued on foot has its advantages, provided you start with a bit of a lead. You can go places where vehicles cannot, and can more easily slip into crowds unnoticed, or hop onto subway cars just as the doors are closing—in time to smirk and wave good-bye. Use the following techniques to stay in the lead and outrun your pursuer, courtesy of former USA National Track and Field Head Coach Mike Fanelli. (Good guys, this is how your bad guys keep evading you until the end of the movie.)

Step 1: Determine whether you will be running for a long distance or a shorter sprint, and use the appropriate technique.

For a short sprint—maximum 500 yards—use explosive power. Exaggerate your gait and lean forward. Use a full arc arm swing and lift your knees high.

For a longer sprint—600 yards to a mile and a half—use maximum efficiency to complete the distance. Use a midfoot plant gait, a lower knee lift, and medium arc arm swing. Lean only slightly forward so that your torso is just ahead of your pelvis.

Step 2: Surge ahead to stay in the lead.

For a controlled distance—whether a short or long sprint—shift into a higher gear to increase your lead. A surge creates distance between you and your pursuer and may help deter him from

Avoid alleys.

Head for crowded areas.

Go to the police station.

Use nearby objects to slow your pursuer.

PACING TIPS

- **Surge around corners. After rounding a corner, with your pursuer out of sight, surge ahead. When he follows he'll discover that your distance has greatly increased.**

- **Surge when your pursuer is hurting. Listen behind you for your pursuer's breathing and pace. When you hear his breathing become labored, pick up the pace.**

pursuing further—he may feel like he has no chance of keeping up. On the other hand, surging for too long can generate lactic acid in your body, which can cause your muscles to tighten and break down your performance.

Step 3: Cut corners to stay in the lead.

Look ahead and take the shortest distance in your path. Take corners by leaning into the angle of the turn. Stay close to the inside of the corner and exaggerate your outside arm arc.

Step 4: Settle into a solid tempo for the straightaways.

Increase your speed slightly to settle into a straightaway. Keep a solid rhythm to maintain your performance. Efficiency is key: Conserve energy for a surge when needed.

Note: Watch your breathing. If it is not labored, you probably have some room to increase your tempo.

Step 5: Head for crowded areas and use bystanders to get between you and your pursuer.

You will be blazing the trail, so try to make it difficult for your pursuer to follow. Tip over garbage cans or food carts to cover your tracks. If your pursuer is in a car, head for a yard or shopping mall—someplace your pursuer can't follow. Run the wrong way down a one-way street.

Miss Moneypenny (Lois Maxwell): *Why are you so late, James?*
James Bond (Roger Moore): *I fell out of an airplane without a parachute.*
   —Moonraker

You know what to do inside a plane to escape—but what do you do outside the plane? In midair? When you don't have a parachute and the only one onboard just left on the bad guy's back? There's only one answer—if you don't have a chute, you'll need to catch up with the person who does. Even if he just left a few seconds earlier. There are two main skydiving positions you'll need to know to accomplish this feat—the boxman and the head-down dive. Both techniques are described below, with instructions from world-record-holding skydiver Mike Zang.

   When you are left in a plane without a parachute, you must act quickly. Once the person with the last parachute has left the plane, follow him out the open door as soon as possible to increase your chances of catching up.

Step 1: Remove loose clothing.
   Remove any articles of clothing that might slow you down by creating drag. But if you have goggles of any sort, put them on—they will help keep wind out of your eyes and improve your visibility.

Step 2: Jump out the airplane door.
   You should jump within 30 seconds of the last person (and last parachute). Any longer than that and you risk not catching him.

Step 3: Move your body into a head-down dive position.

Achieve the head-down dive by facing the earth and making your head the lowest point on your body (i.e., falling face first).

Assume the dive by making the following adjustments to your fall position:

- Point your face to the earth.
  Tilt your head back as far as possible so that your face points down to the earth.
- Extend your body in a straight line behind you.
  Imagine yourself falling to the earth in a straight line—like an arrow.
- Keep your arms and hands straight at your sides.
  Extend your legs and point your toes behind you. Falling in this dive position, a person can reach speeds of up to 200 mph.

Step 4: Spot your target.

Once you find the other person with the chute, don't take your eyes off of him. Follow his "virtual" path with your mind's eye as he falls through cloud cover. He should be falling in a boxman position, the typical "arms and legs spread" skydiving position. He will thus be falling at a slower rate of speed than you are, and will not be looking back or up.

Step 5: Move into position above him.

Using your hands as rudders in the dive position, fall into position directly above him. Extend your right hand by simply bending at the wrist, away from your body, to turn right. Extend your left hand away from your body to turn left.

Step 6: **Move into the boxman position when you are about 30 feet above your target.**

The boxman, or "arched position," is achieved by facing the earth and making your abdomen the lowest point on your body (i.e., falling belly first). Assume the boxman by making the following adjustments to your fall position:

- Face the earth.
- Lean your head back.
- Extend your arms out to the sides, so that they are at a 90-degree angle to your body.
- Bend your legs at the knees and extend them behind you.

Lean back farther and arch your back to increase your speed. The rate of fall in this position can range from 110 to 125 mph.

Step 7: **Fall onto your target and knock him out.**

A body falling to earth creates a burble—a pocket of dead air directly behind it. As you position yourself above your target, you will fall into his burble. This will bring you down directly on top of him with enough force to knock him unconscious.

Step 8: **Grab your target and hook into his harness.**

Chances are that by the time you've caught up with your target and knocked him out, you won't have time to take his chute away from him and put it on—you'll be too close to the ground for this. So you will have to float down together.

Climb around to the front of your target so that you are facing him and wrap your legs around his waist. Extend your right hand between his back and the parachute pack.

Move into the boxman position when 30 feet over your target.
Fall into his burble and render him unconscious—then pull his chute.

Step 9: Release the pilot chute.

With your left hand, release the pilot chute. The pilot chute should be on the right side of the chute pack, at about hip level. It is the small 18-inch chute that pulls the main chute out. As soon as you release the pilot, quickly run your left arm between his back and the parachute pack.

Step 10: Hold on tight.

Hug your target as tightly as possible. Lock your arms and hands together around him. The initial jolt of the parachute deploying can throw you off if you do not hold on tightly.

Step 11: Steer the parachute to the ground.

Pull on the left steering line to go left. Pull on the right to go right.

Step 12: Look for a soft landing spot.

Try to land in the water or on a soft bale of hay—anything that might help to break your fall.

If you've been hitching a ride with the enemy, be sure to bind and gag your flying partner upon landing.

HOW TO CRASH THROUGH A WINDOW

Axel Foley (Eddie Murphy): *Disturbing the peace? I got thrown out of a window! What's the f—ing charge for getting pushed out of a moving car, huh? Jaywalking?!*
    —Beverly Hills Cop

At some point or another, you're going to crash or be thrown through a huge plate glass window. And you will want to know how to survive the experience. The dangers are clear: tempered glass shatters into small pieces that can work their way into smaller areas on your body; untempered glass breaks into larger pieces that cut more easily and may even act like a guillotine when they fall. This can come in handy if you're crashing through a window with the bad guy in tow, but otherwise, it's downright inconvenient. For your safety, we provide the information below, from stuntman Christopher Caso.

GLASS TIPS

- Most office building windows are tempered.

- Modern car windshields are tempered.

- Most residential windows are untempered.

- Most glass in the commercial world is about half an inch thick and in the residential world about a quarter inch or less.

- If you come up against three-quarter-inch glass (used typically for banks, expensive glass tables, or very fancy office buildings), beware—it will be very difficult to break. Try throwing a rock or a chair through first to help shatter the glass. If you are using a chair, a punching motion to the center of the glass is your best shot.

Protect your head, face, and neck.

Punch through the glass.

Lead with your forearms.

Step 1: Quickly run toward the window.

Speed is vital to breaking through any type of glass. For glass thinner than half an inch, you will need to be traveling at least 3 to 5 mph. (For thicker glass, see "Glass Tips," p. 166.)

Step 2: Use your hands and arms to protect your head, face, and neck.

Scrunch your shoulders into your neck. Bring your forearms in front of your neck and face, and bring your hands toward the top of your head.

Step 3: Lead with either a shoulder or your forearms.

If you are breaking through thicker, tempered glass, lead with your shoulder. If you are breaking through thinner, untempered glass, lead with your forearms. Keep your head, face, and neck immediately behind your shoulder or forearms so that they don't linger behind as the glass falls.

Step 4: Break into the glass with a punching motion rather than a flat crash.

Don't just hit the glass dead on. Focus your energy on punching through a specific spot. Once you're through that spot, the rest of the glass will fall like a house of cards.

SKYLIGHTS

- **When jumping through a skylight, lead with your feet. Treat the glass like a pool of water. Jump with your feet together and cover your face with your arms.**
- **When you land, tuck and roll out of the way of the impending shower of glass.**
- **Never look up.**

Step 5: Lean into the direction of the crash.

Keep your arms tight in place and brace for a landing. Close your eyes to avoid cuts on your eyeballs.

Step 6: Stay tucked to hold your landing.

Depending on the thickness of the glass, you will either be thrown backward onto your rear or forward onto your face. Either way, glass will be falling on you. Hold the position of your arms and body to protect yourself from the shattered glass. Roll out of the way if a giant slab of untempered warehouse glass is falling on you; otherwise, stay put.

Step 7: Stand up and brush or shake off the glass before opening your eyes.

HOW TO ESCAPE FROM HANDCUFFS

Harry Tasker (Arnold Schwarzenegger): *I'm going to kill you pretty soon.*
Samir (Charles Cragin): *I see. How exactly?*
Harry: *Well, I thought I'd break your neck, then use you as a human shield, then kill the guard with that knife there on your table and take his gun.*
Samir: *And what makes you think you can do all that?*
Harry: *Because I just picked the lock on these handcuffs . . .*
    —True Lies

There are many different types of handcuffs throughout the world, but the American handcuff is the most commonly used—and the most commonly unlocked. The good news is that handcuffs are designed to be temporary restraints, not permanent ones. So you have a good shot at escape, since American-style cuffs all use a universal key. Remember that you only need to free one hand to restore your mobility—and then dispatch your torturer and his two henchmen. To do so, follow the directions here, provided by escape artist Tom Lyon.

PREPARING FOR ESCAPE

Step 1: As you are being cuffed, tense your wrist muscles.

Tighten or flex your wrist muscles as you are being cuffed. This may allow you more maneuverability later.

Step 2: Try to be left alone.

Ask if you can go to the bathroom or say that you are ill. Ask for a drink or something that would require your guard to leave you unattended.

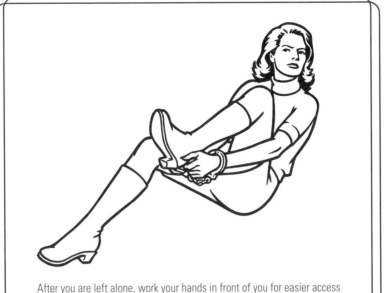

After you are left alone, work your hands in front of you for easier access to the handcuff lock, then attempt to pick the lock.

Step 3: Once alone, work your hands in front of you, if you can.

Though it is possible to escape from handcuffs with your hands behind you, the moves are more difficult. If you can, bring your hands down around your bottom. Slip one hand down, and then the other. Then work both of your hands down toward your feet. Lie on your back and bend your legs. Then, one at a time, bring your feet through the loop of your arms.

PICKING THE LOCK

When you find a tool that you can use as a pick (see step 1) hold it firmly and manipulate it with your thumb and forefinger.

Step 1: Find a pick.

You can pick a handcuff lock relatively easily by bending a resilient piece of metal into the shape of a key. A universal handcuff key is round, with one nodule sticking straight out a few millimeters. Whatever you use, the material must be resilient because the springs on a handcuff lock are strong. Use any of the following items (or your own MacGyveresque creation):

- Large paper clip
- Hairpin
- Mini screwdriver
- Any tough wire (e.g., chicken or piano)
- Small fork
- Electrical wire with the insulation stripped away (10 gauge or higher)
- Thin radio antennae

Step 2: Shape your pick.

Bend a few millimeters of one end of your pick over 90 degrees. This bend should be about the same shape and size as the bit on the end of the universal handcuff key.

Step 3: Put the pick in the lock.

Fit the bend into the lock at the point where the nipple of the key fits. You will feel the bend move into place.

Step 4: Turn the pick to open the lock.

Until you get the feel for what it's like to turn the "key," it may take you a while to pick the lock. Turn your pick left and then right. If you can't get any movement, put the latch end of your handcuff vertically on a hard surface and press down. This may relieve a bit of pressure on the lock and make it easier to turn. Be careful, though: pushing too hard may lock the cuff another tooth and restrict your hand movement.

HIDE A KEY

Because American handcuffs use a universal key, it is a good idea to carry one on your person at all times. You can carry an extra handcuff key (available at any store that carries handcuffs) in your shoe, behind your belt buckle, under your collar, or in a pocket.

Detective John McClane (Bruce Willis) (inside air duct): *Now I know what a TV dinner feels like.*
     —Die Hard

The ventilation system of any large building should provide an excellent escape route in a pinch—albeit a claustrophobic and slightly circuitous one. But when the going gets tough, sometimes the tough have to unscrew a heating vent cover and scurry around like a hamster in a Habitrail to make it out alive. While no HVAC system is the same, there are a few basic principles you can use to escape to safety—as long as you don't end up in the boiler room or get caught in any of those powerful fans. The information here comes from National Air Duct Cleaners Association regional coordinator Edward Frisk.

Step 1: Have a plan.

Before you enter the shaft, try to visualize where you are in the building. Draw a map in your mind of the hallway outside the room you are trying to break into (or out of). This visual map will help you orient yourself in the shaft.

If you have time to access the blueprints of the building, use them to map your route. Most building maintenance offices store these blueprints, and they are usually left unguarded. Slip into the office, locate the blueprints, and make a quick sketch of your route.

Step 2: **Remove the vent cover of, preferably, a cold air return duct.**

If you are entering a system at the furnace or conditioning unit, you'll notice that the cold air return cover plates are typically larger than those providing output air. Hold a lit match in front of the grate. If the flame is drawn into the grate, then you have found a cold air return. If the flame is blown out—away from the grate—then you have found a supply line vent.

AIR RETURN VARIETIES

Most office buildings will have a ducted return, but occasionally you'll come into contact with an "open plenum return." These returns simply draw air from the space between the ceiling and the main return shaft. If you encounter this system, backtrack through the ductwork to the beginning. Your only other option will be to enter the system's supply lines.

Supply line ducts can be entered as well—although they are typically smaller than return ducts. These are the output legs of the ventilation system. Treat them as you would a cold air return leg. Work the screws loose and remove the cover plate quietly. Be sure to hold the grate against the wall so that you do not drop it when the screws come out. If you do not have a small screwdriver, try a thin coin or the end of a paper clip. Carefully place the cover on the floor.

Step 3: **Enter the shaft head first, and head toward the back of the building.**

Some ventilation system exits terminate in the basement or on the roof, and are usually at the back of the building. Some, however, are restricted by floor—that is, each floor has its own self-contained system. If this is the case—and you'll know if you cannot travel from floor to floor—remain in the ventilation system until the coast is clear before climbing out to make your escape. If the system is not floor-restricted, and you know which floor of the building you are on, determine whether you are closer to the roof or the basement and head that way.

Step 4: Equalize your weight when you crawl horizontally.
Most ventilation systems are held in place with sheet metal straps (typically rated to 200 pounds). When crawling through the ventilation line, keep your weight distributed as evenly as possible from front to back to prevent breakage in a joint. As you move forward, be sure to keep some weight on your legs. Sliding rather than crawling will help you achieve this.

OBSTACLES

You are likely to encounter turning vanes or dampers ("fins" made of sheet metal) within the ductwork as you crawl. They are designed to decrease and direct airflow within a ventilation system (especially at the 90-degree bends). At first sight, they seem to completely block your passage, but they can prove to be helpful tools.

Remove the turning vanes and dampers. They can be slid out by hand, or knocked out with a swift kick. Take a fin with you. Fold one in half to make a pry bar, or save one as is—its sharp edges make it a valuable weapon.

Step 5: Use the grates you pass along the way to orient yourself further.
Peek through the grates to determine where you are.

Step 6: If you encounter a drop in the shaft, climb down—do not jump.
Place your back against one wall and your feet against the other. Keep pressure on your back and feet at all times, then lower one leg, then your back, then the other leg as you descend—

essentially wedging yourself between the sides of the shaft. Keep your hands on the walls to help control your drop. Move them down in turn.

Step 7: Look for an empty room or closet to exit the shaft.
When you reach a grate in a room you believe is safe enough to attempt an escape from, remove the screws from behind or pry them off with your makeshift fin. Hold onto the grate so that it doesn't fall and make a loud ruckus. (Slip a shoelace or your belt through one of the holes and back again if you cannot hold the grate with your fingers.)

Step 8: Climb out of the vent and make your escape.
After you emerge from the vent (and have made sure the coast is clear), be sure to rifle through any filing cabinets that may have valuable information.

NAVIGATING TIPS

- **When traveling through supply line branches, do not worry if the heat comes on. Temperatures are not high enough to cause burns.**

- **When traveling though cold air return ducts, try not to kick up dust. Some unmaintained lines can have a half-inch of dirt in them. Slide across these piles slowly so as not to reveal your position.**

- **An average-size person should be able to move fairly freely through a 16" x 25" duct. Access into smaller ducts may be limited depending on your size.**

HOW TO ESCAPE
A SINKING CRUISE SHIP

Rose DeWitt Bukater (Kate Winslet): *So this is the ship they say is unsinkable.*
Cal Hockley (Billy Zane): *It is unsinkable. God himself couldn't sink this ship.*
—*Titanic*

Fortunately, today's action hero doesn't have to contend with the limited number of lifeboats or the class restrictions established by the White Star Line. Still, you should know what to do in the water and how to get far enough away from the vacuum effect created by a sinking ship. Ninety-nine times out of a hundred, when you find yourself on a sinking ship, you should obey the ship's officers' instructions. Above all, remain calm—and try not to get handcuffed to a pipe in the lower decks. The information here comes from Captain Cynthia Lynn Smith, professor of nautical sciences.

BEFORE THE SHIP DEPARTS

- Pack the right survival gear, just in case.

  A little preparation goes a long way, so bring the following:
    - Long-sleeved, light-colored cotton shirt (for easier spotting by rescue crews)
    - Light-colored cotton baseball hat
    - Flashlight
    - Sunscreen (40+ SPF)
    - Water bottle
    - Loose, light cotton pants (sweatpants)
    - Flat shoes with good grip soles

- Make sure your cabin has its own personal flotation device (PFD). Check in the closet or under the bed. A device should be clearly marked.

  Practice putting it on correctly. Also, check to see that all of the survival tools on it—whistle, light, straps—work. Be sure to check the expiration date and have the PFD replaced immediately if it has expired.

- Locate the two nearest lifeboats or life rafts.

  Your cabin should not be far from one. If it is, ask to be reassigned to a cabin in closer proximity to such craft. Alternatively, reserve a cabin near the embarkation deck, near a weather door.

- Store your emergency survival gear in the open with your PFD, for easy access in case of emergency.

IF THE SHIP STARTS SINKING

If you hear seven or more short blasts from the ship's whistle, seven or more blasts of the general alarm, a continuous sounding of the ship's whistle, or if the ship lists to one side and does not correct itself, your ship is most likely sinking.

Step 1: Go to your cabin and get your PFD.

If time permits, grab your supplies from your cabin. Bring all of your survival gear.

Step 2: Calmly move to your lifeboat and follow the orders of the crewmember in charge.

Emergency exits and stairwells should be lit. Look for the lights marking these exits on the way to the lifeboats.

Step 3: Remain calm and do not jump into the water or the lower deck unless you have no other choice.

Most ships sink slowly, so it will not be necessary to jump. Wait until you can board a lifeboat and remain calm.

Step 4: If you have to jump, look before you leap.

Do not jump onto a lower deck, into a lifeboat, or onto other people below you. Jump feet-first from as low a point as possible, as close to the water as you can get. Try to jump as far from the boat as possible, and hold your PFD at the top of the vest so that it won't ride up on your neck.

Step 5: Swim away from the boat as soon as you hit the water.

Otherwise, you may be sucked under by the vacuum effect created as the ship goes down.

Step 6: Try to find a lifeboat or something to float on as soon as possible.
You have a much better chance of surviving if you are even partially out of the water than if you are immersed.

Step 7: If no lifeboat or raft is reachable, float in a group with other survivors.
The shared body warmth will help keep you all warm, and you will be able to encourage each others' survival.

Step 8: Kick or punch at anything that brushes you from below.
Sharks may come around at dusk for feeding—so be on your guard, and fight back. Kick, poke, or punch them in the eyes or gills if you can. Most will back off.

Roger Thornhill (Cary Grant): *This is no good, we're on top of the monument!*
Eve Kendall (Eva Marie Saint): *What'll we do?*
Roger: *Climb down.*
   —*North by Northwest*

It happens sometimes—you're mistaken for a secret agent and you follow your ingénue to the bad guy's hideout atop Mount Rushmore. Once you've retrieved the microfilm and the ingénue, you'll need to know how to safely make your descent down the face of the monument. Without the proper gear, you will need to rely on strength, technique, and the instructions below for the best route down. So commit this to memory, take a deep breath, and whatever happens, hang onto the ingénue. These instructions are brought to you by champion climbers Jason and Tiffany Campbell.

TECHNIQUE

Use the following climbing techniques to descend.

Step 1: Use the proper grips.

Depending on the hold available, use one of the following grips.

- *The pinch.* Use on vertical holds or cracks. Rotate your hand as if you were going to grab a flagpole. Depending on the features of the hold, set your fingers so that your strongest fingers—typically index and forefinger—have the best grip. Close your thumb on the other side of the hold and press it toward your fingers so that it pinches the hold. It is best to move away from this hold (e.g., with a left hand hold, move down and right).

- *The crimp.* Use on horizontal divots, pockmarks, and other features. Grab the hold with your four fingertips in a tight line. Wrap your thumb over your index finger. Your fingertips will be performing the grip while your thumb provides an almost "locking" support to the rest of your hand.

Step 2: Do not panic.

In order for you to make your descent, you will need to conserve all your strength and energy—so remain in the proper mindset. Keep breathing. Give yourself positive affirmations like "you can do it," and "keep moving." Remember that fear is the mind killer.

Step 3: Down-climb on the more featured rock (hair, sideburns, eyes).

Where the rock is more textured with divots and holds, use the down-climbing technique. Facing the rock with both hands and both feet supporting your weight, move your limbs one at a time. Lower a hand onto another hold. Once you've grasped it, lower your opposite foot to another hold. Continue down-climbing as long as you can grip the features on the rock.

Step 4: Friction climb on the smoother rock (cheeks, lips, chins, and necks).

Face the rock and get on all fours. Using the grip of your shoes, lift your heels up high off the wall so that your weight is on your hands and the balls of your feet. Stick your rear out so that you are pressed into the rock. Press and "rub" or "twist" your foot into a divot hold. Use the friction to hold your weight as you lower yourself down the rock. If there is not another divot close by, spot one a short distance below. Moving very slowly and deliberately, slide down to the divot and catch your weight on your foot. DO NOT LET YOURSELF SLIDE TOO FAST OR YOU WILL FALL.

Follow this route down the monument:

Step 5: Rest in an outcropping or ear.

When you have a ledge to stand on, come to a rest. Facing outward, rest the balls of your feet by standing on your heels and leaning your head back to the rock. Shake out your hands, arms, legs, and feet.

THE ROUTE

The best way down is the path with the most features and textured rock—this will be easier to climb on, since you'll have more holds.

Step 1: Work your way from Jefferson's hair down to the left of his ear.
You will have to use a combination of both down-climbing and friction-climbing techniques.

Step 2: Lower yourself slowly to Washington's chin.

Step 3: Traverse under Washington's chin and across Jefferson's neck.

Step 4: Arrive between Roosevelt and Lincoln on the down slope just above the trees.
This area is much less steep, so you should be able to walk a zigzag pattern down the hill the rest of the way.

Warning: If at any point during your descent you fall, let your body fall limp. This may help you absorb the impact and leave you with fewer injuries.

Chapter 1—Good Guy Skills

How to Secure/Spyproof a Hotel Room—Shawn Engbrecht is one of the world's top protection officers, with years of experience working in high-risk areas, including Colombia, Ecuador, Peru, and the former USSR. When not on operational assignment, he is the primary instructor at the Center for Advanced Security Studies in Naples, Florida, one of the premiere bodyguard training facilities in the commercial sector.

How to Secure and Read a Crime Scene—George Throckmorton is the manager of the SLPD Crime Lab, specializing in fingerprint and questionable document identifications. After training with the F.B.I. and Secret Service, George taught scientific investigative techniques at Washington State University, American Express Corp., and the Florida Police Academy. Kevin Patrick teaches crime scene investigation throughout the United States. He is the director of the Utah Crime Scene Academy, the supervising criminalist of the identification section of the Utah State Crime Lab, and supervisor of the state's Crime Scene Response Team.

How to Take Fingerprints—George Throckmorton.

How to Track a Fugitive—Kevin R. Hackie owned and operated a bail recovery school in California. He was a bounty hunter and police officer for 20 years, and is now the CEO of Beach Cities Protective Services.

How to Interrogate a Suspect—Detective Chip Morgan is a criminal polygraph examiner and trainer. For more than 20 years, Detective Morgan has shared his training and expertise with others in the law enforcement arena.

How to Survive in Prison When You're Wrongfully Incarcerated—In 1973 Mike Pardue, at age 17, was wrongfully imprisoned. He was freed on February 15, 2001, after 27 years and nine months of illegal incarceration. He presently lives in freedom and joy with his wife and soul mate, Becky.

How to Catch a Great White Shark—Douglas Mizzi has been shark fishing since 1992. He is the owner of the Web site Land Based Shark Fishing Australia & International. He was taught his technique by good friend and shark hunter Vic Hislop.

How to Tell When Someone Is Really Dead—Andrew J. Michaels, M.D., M.P.H., F.A.C.S., is a trauma surgeon and the Director of General Surgical Trauma Services at Legacy/Emanuel Hospital in Portland, Oregon. He is also a clinical associate professor of surgery at Oregon Health Sciences University.

How to Save Someone Who Has Flat-Lined—Andrew J. Michaels, M.D., M.P.H., F.A.C.S.

How to Drive a Bus at High Speed—Bob Tyree has been driving a bus for 25 years and nearly two million miles. He has spent many years as an accident review committee member for the Amalgamated Transit Union.

How to Negotiate a Hostage Crisis—Sgt. Larry J. Chavez, B.A., M.P.A., is a 30-year law enforcement veteran and senior hostage negotiator for the Sacramento Police Department. A graduate of the F.B.I. Hostage Negotiations School at Quantico, Virginia, he has authored and published several articles on hostage negotiation and workplace violence awareness and prevention.

How to Take a Bullet—Shawn Engbrecht.

How to Save Someone from Being Hit by a Speeding Car—Christopher Caso is a stuntman and member of both the U.C.L.A. and U.S. gymnastics teams. He has performed stunts in such films as *Spider-Man*, *The One*, and *The Lost World*.

How to Save Someone Who's Hanging from a Cliff—Christopher Caso.

Chapter 2—Love Skills

How to Stop a Wedding—Sara L. Ambarian has worked in the wedding industry since the mid-1980s as a custom bridal designer and creative wedding consultant. She is the author of *A Bride's Touch: A Handbook of Wedding Personality and Inspiration*, and a contributor to wedding Web sites in the United States, Canada, and Australia. She also publishes her own wedding information Web site at www.frazmtn.com/~ambarian.

How to Dirty Dance—Cynthia Fleming has served as choreographer for a variety of theatre productions, trade shows, and tributes. She performed in *A Chorus Line* in the Broadway, international, and national companies.

How to Make and Use a Love Potion—Gerina Dunwich is a practicing witch, professional astrologer, ordained minister, and spokesperson for the magical community. She is the author of more than 20 books on witchcraft and the occult arts.

How to Pick Someone Up in a Bar—Craig Lowe is a longtime bartender, stock trader, and Web designer. His Web site, www.bartendersview.com, is dedicated to the bartending life.

How to Turn Sexual Tension into Mad, Passionate Sex—Dr. Carol Queen is staff sexologist at Good Vibrations, the Bay Area's women-owned, worker-owned sex shop. She writes regularly for their Web magazine at www.goodvibes.com, and has several books in print, including *Exhibitionism for the Shy*. Visit her Web site at www.carolqueen.com.

Chapter 3—Paranormal Skills

How to Communicate with an Extraterrestial—John Elliott, B.Sc., M.Sc., Ph.D, is a research student at the Center for Computer Analysis of Language and Speech at the School of Computing, University of Leeds, England. Aims of this research include the detection of language-like features in signals to aid the deciphering of unknown languages and identify extraterrestrial intelligence.

How to Contact the Dead—Tracey has been delving in the medium arts since childhood and has spent the last 26 years formally studying them. She is a master of tarot, an expert on various forms of medium and divination arts, and has taught the predictive sciences to others through the School of Medium Arts. She is the author of *Tarot and the Old Testament*, and can be contacted at www.tarotbytracey.com.

How to Fend Off a Ghost—Tracey.

How to Predict the Future—Tracey.

How to Perform the Jedi Mind Trick—Known as "The World's Fastest Hypnotist," Spencer has been practicing since 1969. He has trained more than 20,000 people in hypnosis, produced a radio talk show, and been featured on Playboy TV. You can catch Spencer at www.sleepnow.com or visit his ongoing hypnosis show in Las Vegas.

How to Perform the Vulcan Nerve Pinch—Ray Geraneo is the founder of Kenka Karate. Nationally recognized as a martial arts innovator, he is a Hall of Fame member of the World Head of Family Sokeship Council, a defensive tactics instructor, and a member of the American Society of Law Enforcement Training.

Chapter 4—Fighting Skills

How to Train for a World Championship Title Fight—Cappy Kotz owns Cappy's on Union Boxing Gym in Seattle, Washington, and is author of *Boxing for Everyone: How to Get Fit and Have Fun with Boxing*.

How to Take a Hit with a Chair—Christopher Caso.

How to Draw and Win a Gunfight—Howard Darby is the 2000 and 2001 All-Around Fast Draw World Champion, and holds 14 world records in the sport of fast draw. He has been competing in fast draw for more than 20 years.

How to Be Ready for Anything—Andrew Netschay is the founder of Confrontation Management Systems. His experience spans over 17 years of intensive training and research, working with Fortune 500 executives, law enforcement officers, professional athletes, and survivors of violent crime and assault. He wrote and produced the three-part TV series *Street Defense: Empowerment Strategies*, and is considered an authority on negotiation, empowerment, and safety strategies.

How to Win a Fight When You're Outnumbered—Ray Geraneo.

How to Disarm a Thug with a Gun—Shawn Engbrecht.

Chapter 5—Escape Skills

How to Evade a MiG—Walt Addison Linscott is a professional air show and television/motion picture production stunt pilot based in Atlanta, Georgia. One of the few pilots in the world authorized to perform acrobatic flight without altitude limitation, he has amassed more than 10,000 flight hours in a wide variety of aircraft. Visit his Web site at www.paramountaerobatics.com.

How to Fix Your Space Shuttle on Reentry—Lisa B. Shore works at the Johnson Space Center as a flight dynamics officer in the Mission Control Center. She previously worked with the United Space Alliance during the *Challenger* disaster.

How to Make a Clean Getaway—Shawn Engbrecht.

How to Win a High-Speed Car Chase—Vinny Minchillo is an amateur racer, demolition derby driver, and fan of all things automotive. When he isn't behind the wheel, he's a creative director for Temerlin McClain Advertising in Irving, Texas. His work has appeared in car magazines including *Auto Week* and *Sports Car*, and on the NPR radio program *Imagination Workshop.*

How to Win a High-Speed Chase on Foot—Mike Fanelli was appointed the head coach of the U.S. National Track and Field Team in 1992, 1996, and 2000. He has also coached 15 Olympic trial qualifiers and run nearly 50 races, from the marathon to the 100-mile race.

How to Catch Someone in the Air When You Don't Have a Parachute—Michael J. Zang began skydiving in 1991. He has made more than 3,700 skydives and holds the world record for the most skydives in 24 hours (500). As a pilot, Michael has accumulated more than 5,500 hours of flight time.

How to Crash Through a Window—Christopher Caso.

How to Escape from Handcuffs—Tom Lyon is a U.K. escape artist who has been escaping from handcuffs, locks, and straightjackets since the age of seven.

How to Navigate a Ventilation Shaft—Edward Frisk is the vice-president and general manager of Ductworks, Inc., of Colorado. He is the regional coordinator of the National Air Duct Cleaners Association (www.ductworks.com), overseeing six western states.

How to Escape a Sinking Cruise Ship—Captain Cynthia Lynn Smith is a professor of nautical sciences in the Department of Marine Transportation at the United States Merchant Marine Academy in Kings Point, New York, where she teaches courses in celestial, terrestrial, and electronic navigation, ship handling, firefighting, seamanship, and survival at sea. She is a Master Mariner, licensed to sail vessels of any tonnage on any ocean.

How to Climb Down Mount Rushmore—Professional rock climbers Jason and Tiffany Campbell are experts in stunt work, rigging, wall design, and coaching. They are national climbing champions with X-Games medals and numerous first ascents up to 5.14C-graded climbs, and are certified competition course setters. Their indoor/outdoor ProClimb LLC workshops are based in Las Vegas (www.proclimbing.com).

ABOUT THE AUTHORS

David Borgenicht is the co-author of the *New York Times* best-selling *Worst-Case Scenario Survival Handbooks* (Chronicle). Despite his extensive survival knowledge, he has yet to save the world from destruction. He is, however, pretty good at basic home repair and CPR. He is also the co-author, with his brother, Joe, of the not-so-best-selling but lengthily titled *Mom Always Said "Don't Play Ball in the House" and Other Stuff We Learned from TV* (Chilton). He lives in Philadelphia with his wife and daughter—who save him from insanity almost daily.

Joe Borgenicht is a writer and producer who has co-authored several books, including *Mom Always Said "Don't Play Ball in the House" and Other Stuff We Learned from TV* (Chilton) and *Doggy Days* (Ten Speed). He has caught a small but very mean red snapper in the somewhat deep waters of the Caribbean, won a high-speed chase in a car and then lost a high-speed chase on foot, and disarmed a cousin with a cap gun (sorry Casey, I meant to kick you in the stomach). He lives in Salt Lake City, Utah, with his wife, son, and dog.

ACKNOWLEDGMENTS

David Borgenicht would like to thank the following people: His brother, Joe, who did all the real work; Mindy Brown, who worked many long nights editing this manuscript to make this book happen (your boss should give you a raise); Frances Soo Ping Chow, who also worked many long nights designing this manuscript to make this book happen (your boss should give you a raise, too); Larry Jost, who did a fabulous job illustrating this book (and probably also worked many long nights to make this book happen); and everyone else at Quirk and Chronicle Books, without whom this would not have been possible or even seemed like a good idea. He also thanks Sean Connery, Clint Eastwood, Bruce Willis, Harrison Ford, and Arnold Schwarzenegger for their inspiration. Finally, a very special thanks to the real action heroes of this book—the experts whose knowledge made it real.

Joe Borgenicht would like to thank all of the experts who contributed their experience to this book—this would not have been possible without you. He would like to thank his brother and co-author, David, for always taking the "w" out of *work* (yes, we get paid for doing this). He would like to thank the best editor in the world, Mindy Brown at Quirk Books—you always know how to get a f—ing answer! Thanks to Quirk Books, Frances, and Larry—without you it's just worms, Roxanne, worms. He would also like to thank Sean, Roger, Arnie, Sly, Harrison, Bruce, Jamie Lee, Keanu, Tommy Lee, Wesley, Nicolas, Kevin, Samuel L., Diane, J, Dustin, Patrick, Sandra, Linda, Sean, Richard, Roy, Bill, Harold, Mark, Alec, Leonard, Emilio, Jackie, Chris, Tom, Ed, Cary, Clint, and all the other action heroes who inspired and followed them. He would like to thank his mother, Nancy, for introducing him to movie magic by getting killed in *Halloween 4* and *Silent Night, Deadly Night*—and then one last time in the sequel. Finally, he would like to thank the two greatest heroes in his life, his wife, Melanie, and son, Jonah "Bugs"—I cherish you, your support, your love, and your drool.